Talismanic Magic And The

Composition Of Talismans

L. W. de Laurence

Kessinger Publishing's Rare Reprints

Thousands of Scarce and Hard-to-Find Books on These and other Subjects!

- Americana
- Ancient Mysteries
- Animals
- Anthropology
- Architecture
- Arts
- Astrology
- Bibliographies
- Biographies & Memoirs
- Body, Mind & Spirit
- Business & Investing
- Children & Young Adult
- Collectibles
- Comparative Religions
- Crafts & Hobbies
- Earth Sciences
- Education
- Ephemera
- Fiction
- Folklore
- Geography
- Health & Diet
- History
- Hobbies & Leisure
- Humor
- Illustrated Books
- Language & Culture
- Law
- Life Sciences
- Literature
- Medicine & Pharmacy
- Metaphysical
- Music
- Mystery & Crime
- Mythology
- Natural History
- Outdoor & Nature
- Philosophy
- Poetry
- Political Science
- Science
- Psychiatry & Psychology
- Reference
- Religion & Spiritualism
- Rhetoric
- Sacred Books
- Science Fiction
- Science & Technology
- Self-Help
- Social Sciences
- Symbolism
- Theatre & Drama
- Theology
- Travel & Explorations
- War & Military
- Women
- Yoga
- *Plus Much More!*

**We kindly invite you to view our catalog list at:
http://www.kessinger.net**

CHAPTER VI.

Talismanic Magic.

THE COMPOSITION OF TALISMANS.

TALISMANIC OPERATIONS.

Man should study the Metaphysical *causes*,
Which underlie all physical *effects;*
He should pierce not only the causes,
But master the Occult and Spiritual forces,
Which are the controlling influences of
His physical, mental, and moral *existence*.

IT is necessary that the student should know and understand the nature and quality of the *Four Elements*, in order to be perfect in the principles and ground-work of his studies in *Talismanic Magic*.

Therefore, there are four elements, the original grounds of all corporeal things, viz. fire, earth, water, and air, of which elements all inferior bodies are compounded; not by way of being heaped up together, but by transmutation and union; and when they are destroyed, they are resolved into elements. But there are none of the sensible elements that are pure; but they are, more or less, mixed, and apt to be changed the one into the other; even as earth, being moistened and dissolved, becomes *water*, but the same being made thick and hard becomes earth again; and being evaporated through heat it passes into air, and that being kindled into fire, and this being extinguished, into air again, but being cooled after burning, becomes earth again, or else stone or sulphur; and this is clearly demonstrated by lightning. Now every one of these elements have two specific properties: the former whereof it retains as proper to itself; in the other, as a mean, it agrees with that which comes directly after it. For fire is hot and dry—earth, cold and dry;—water, cold and moist—and air, hot and moist. And so in this manner the elements, according to two contrary qualities, are opposite one to the other: as fire to water, and earth to air. Likewise, the elements are contrary one to the other on another account: two are heavy, as earth and water—and the others are light, as fire and air; therefore the Stoics called the former, passives—but the latter, actives. The Lamas distinguish them after another manner, and assigns to each of them three qualities, viz. to the fire, brightness, thinness, and motion—to the earth,

127

darkness, thickness, and quietness; and, according to these qualities, the elements of fire and earth are contrary. Now the other elements borrow their qualities from these, so that the air receives two qualities from the fire,—thinness and motion; and the earth one, viz. darkness. In like manner water receives two qualities of the earth,—darkness and thickness; and the fire one, viz. motion. But fire is twice as thin as air, thrice more moveable, and four times brighter; the air is twice more bright, thrice more thin, and four times more movable. Therefore, as fire is to air, so is air to water, and water to the earth; and again, as the earth is to the water, so is water to air, and air to fire. And this is the root and foundation of all bodies, natures, and wonderful works; and he who can know, and thoroughly understand these qualities of the elements, and their mixtures, shall bring to pass wonderful and astonishing things in Magic.

Now each of these elements have a threefold consideration, so that the number of four may make up the number of twelve; and, by passing by the number of seven into ten, there may be a progress to the supreme unity upon which all virtue and wonderful things do depend. Of the first order are the pure elements, which are neither compounded, changed, or mixed, but are incorruptible; and not OF which, but *through* which, the virtues of all natural things are brought forth to act. No man is able fully to declare their virtues, because they can do all things upon all things. He who remains ignorant of these, shall never be able to bring to pass any wonderful matter.

Of the second order are elements that are compounded, changeable, and impure; yet such as may, by Art, be reduced to their pure simplicity; whose virtue, when they are thus reduced, doth, above all things, perfect all occult and common operations of Nature; and these are the foundation of the whole of *Natural Magic*.

Of the third order, are those elements which originally and of themselves are not elements, but are twice compounded, various and changeable into another. These are the infallible *medium*, and are called the *middle nature*, or soul of the middle nature; very few there are that understand the deep mysteries thereof. In them is, by means of certain numbers, degrees, and orders, the perfection of every effect in what thing soever, whether *natural, celestial*, or supercelestial: they are full of wonders and mysteries, and are operative as in Magic natural, so divine. For from these, through them, proceeds the binding, loosing, and transmutation of all things—the knowledge and foretelling of things to come—also, the expelling of evil, and the gaining of good spirits. Let no one, therefore, without these three sorts of elements, and the true knowledge thereof, be confident that he can work any thing in Nature and Natural Magic.

But whosoever shall know how to reduce those of one order into another, impure into pure, compounded into single, and shall understand distinctly the *nature, virtue,* and power of them, in number, degrees, and order, without dividing the substance, he shall easily attain to the knowledge and perfect operation of all natural things, and celestial secrets likewise; and this is the perfection of the *Cabala,* which teaches all these before mentioned; and, by a perfect knowledge thereof, I perform many rare and wonderful experiments.

PROPERTIES AND NATURE OF FIRE AND EARTH.

Of the Elements.   There are two things, viz. fire and earth, which are sufficient for the operation of all wonderful things: the former is active and the latter passive.   Fire, in all things, and through all things, comes and goes away bright; it is in all things bright, and at the same time Occult and unseen.   When it is by itself (no other matter coming to it, in which it should manifest its proper action) it is boundless and invisible; of itself sufficient for every action that is proper to it;—itself is one, and penetrates through all things; also spread abroad in the heavens, and shining.   But in the infernal place, straitened, dark, and tormenting; and in the midway it partakes of both.   It is in stones, and is drawn out by the stroke of the steel; it is in earth, and causes it, after digging up, to smoke; it is in water, and heats springs and wells; it is in the depths of the sea, and causes it, being tossed with the winds, to be hot; it is in the air, and makes it (as we often see) to burn.   And all animals, and all living things whatsoever, as also vegetables are preserved by heat;—and everything that lives, lives by reason of the inclosed heat.   The properties of the fire that is above, are heat, making all things fruitful; and a celestial light, giving life to all things.   The properties of the infernal fire are a parching heat, consuming all things; and darkness; making all things barren.   The celestial and bright fire drives away spirits of darkness;—also, this our fire, made with wood, drives away the same, in as much as it hath an analogy with, and is the *vehiculum* of that superior light; as also of him who saith, "I am the light of the world," which is true fire—the Father of lights, from whom every good thing that is given comes;—sending forth the light of his fire, and communicating it first to the sun and the rest of the celestial bodies, and by these, as by mediating instruments, conveying that light into our fire.   As, therefore, the spirits of darkness are stronger in the dark—so good spirits, which are angels of lights, are augmented not only by that light (which is divine, of the sun, and celestial), but also by the light of our common fire.   Hence it was that the first and most wise institutors of religions and ceremonies, ordained that prayers, singings, and all manner of divine worships whatsoever, should not be performed without lighted candles or torches; hence, also, was that sig-

nificant saying of the Lamas—"Do not speak of God without a light!"
—And they commanded that, for the driving away of wicked spirits,
lights and fires should be kindled by the carcasses of the dead, and that
they should not be removed until the expiations were, after a holy manner, performed, and then buried.   And the great Jehovah himself, in
the old law, commanded that all his sacrifices should be offered with fire
and that fire should always be burning upon the altar, which custom the
Priests of the Altar did always observe and keep amongst the Romans.
Now the basis and foundation of all the elements is the earth; for that
is the object, subject and receptacle of all celestial rays and influences:
in it are contained the seeds, and seminal virtues of all things: and
therefore, it is said to be animal, vegetable, and mineral.   It, being
made fruitful by the other elements and the heavens, brings forth all
things of itself.   It receives the abundance of all things, and is, as it
were, the first fountain from whence all things spring;—it is the centre,
foundation, and mother of all things.   Take as much of it as you please,
separated, washed, depurated, and subtilized, and if you let it lie in
the open air a little while, it will, being full and abounding with heavenly
virtues, of itself bring forth plant, worms, and other living things; also
stones, and bright sparks of *metals*.   In it are great secrets: if, at any
time it shall be purified, by the help of fire,* and reduced into its simple
nature by a convenient washing, it is the first matter of our creation,
and the truest medicine that can restore and preserve us.

The other two elements, viz. water and air, are not less efficacious
than the former; neither is Nature wanting to work wonderful things
in them.   There is so great a necessity of water, that without it nothing
can live—no herb, no plant whatsoever without the moistening of
water, can bring forth; in it is the seminary virtue of all things, especially of animals, whose seed is manifestly waterish.   The seeds, also,
of trees and plants, although they are earthy, must, notwithstanding,
of necessity be rotted in water before they can be fruitful; whether
they be imbibed with the moisture of the earth, or with dew, or rain,
or any other water that is on purpose put to them.—For Moses writes,
that only earth and water can bring forth a living soul; but he ascribes
a two-fold production of things to water, viz. of things swimming in
the water, and of things flying in the air above the earth; and that those
productions that are made in and upon the earth are partly attributed
to the very water the same scripture testifies, where it saith, that the
plants and the herbs did not grow, because God had not caused it to
rain upon the earth.   Such is the efficacy of this element of water, that

---

*The author here, speaking of the element of earth being reduced to its utmost
simplicity, by being purified by fire and a convenient washing, means, that it is the
first and principal ingredient necessary to the production of the Philosopher's
stone, either of animals or metals.

spiritual regeneration cannot be done without it, as Christ himself testified to Nicodemus.   Very great, also, is the virtue of it in religious worship, in expiations and purifications; indeed, the necessity of it is no less than that of fire.   Infinite are the benefits, indeed the necessity of it is no less than that of fire.   Infinite are the benefits, and divers are the uses, thereof as being that, by virtue of which all things subsist, are generated, nourished, and increased.   Hence it was that Thales of Miletus, and Hesiod, concluded that water was the beginning of all things; and said it was the first of all the elements, and the most potent; and that, because it hath the mastery over all the rest. For, as the Adept saith,—"Waters swallow up the earth—extinguish flames—ascend on high—and, by the stretching forth of the clouds, challenge the heavens for their own; the same, falling down, becomes the cause of all things that grow in the earth."   Very many are the wonders that are done by waters, according to the teachings of the Hindu Adepts.

Josephus also makes relation of the wonderful nature of a certain river betwixt *Arcea* and *Raphanea,* cities of *Syria,* which runs with a full channel all the Sabbath-day, and then on a sudden stops, as if the springs were stopped, and all the six days you may pass over it dry-shod; but again, on the seventh day, no man knowing the reason of it, the waters return again, in abundance as before! wherefore the inhabitants thereabout called it the Sabbath-day River, because of the seventh day, which was holy to the Jews.—The Gospel, also, testifies of a sheep-pool, into which whosoever stepped first after the water was troubled by the Angel, was made whole of whatsoever disease he had.   This same virtue and efficacy, we read, was in a spring of the *Ionian Nymphs,* which was in the territories belonging to the town of *Elis,* at a village called *Heradea,* near the river *Citheron,* which whosoever stepped into, being diseased, came forth whole, and cured of all his diseases.   *Pausanias* also reports, that in Lyceus, a mountain of Arcadia, there was a spring called *Agria,* to which, as often as the dryness of the region threatened the destruction of fruits, *Jupiter, Priest* of *Lyceus,* went; and, after the offering of sacrifices, devoutly praying to the waters of the spring, holding a bough of an oak in his hand, put it down to the bottom of the hallowed spring; then, the waters being troubled, a vapor ascending from thence into the air, was blown into clouds, which being joined together, the whole heaven was overspread: which being, a little after, dissolved into rain, watered all the country most wholesomely.—Moreover, *Ruffus, a* physician of *Ephesus,* besides many other authors, wrote strange things concerning the wonders of waters, which, for aught I know, are found in no other author.

It remains, that I speak of the air.—This is a vital spirit passing through all beings—giving life and subsistence to all things—moving and filling all things.   Hence it is that the Hindus Yoghees reckon it not amongst the elements; but count it as a medium, or glue, joining things together, and as the resounding spirit of the world's instrument. It immediately receives into itself the influence of all celestial bodies, and then communicates them to the other elements, as also to all mixed bodies.   Also, it receives into itself, as if it were a divine looking-glass, the species of all things, as well natural as artificial; as also of all manner of speeches, and retains them; and carrying them with it, and entering into the bodies of men, and other animals, through their pores, makes an impression upon them, as well when they are asleep as when they are awake, and affords matter for divers strange dreams and divinations.—Hence it is that a man, passing by a place where a man was slain, or the carcass newly hid, is moved with fear and dread; because the air, in that place, being full of the dreadful species of man-slaughter, doth, being breathed in, move and trouble the spirit of the man with the like species; whence it is that he becomes afraid.   For everything that makes a sudden impression affects the soul.   Whence it is that many philosophers were of opinion, that air is the cause of dreams, and of many other impressions of the mind, through the pro-longing of images, or similitudes, or species (which proceed from things and speeches, multiplied in the very air), until they come to the senses, and then to the phantasy and soul of him that receives them; which, being freed from cares, and no way hindered, expecting to meet such kind of species, is informed by them.   For the species of things, although of their own proper nature they are carried to the senses of men, and other animals in general, may, notwithstanding, get some impression from the heavens whilst they are in the air; by reason of which, together with the aptness and disposition of him that receives them, they may be carried to the sense of one, rather than of another.   And hence it is possible, naturally, and far from all manner of superstition (no other spirit coming between), that a man should be able, in a very small time, to signify his mind unto another telepathy man, abiding at a very long and unknown distance from him—although he cannot precisely give an estimate of the time, when it is, yet of necessity, it must be within twenty-four hours;—and I, myself, know how to do it, and have often done it.   The same also, in time past, did the Adepts and both know and do.—Also, when certain appearances (not only spiritual, but also natural) do flow forth from things, that is to say, by a certain kind of flowings forth of bodies from bodies, and do gather strength in the air, they shew themselves to us as well through light as motion—as well to the sight as to other senses—and sometimes work wonderful things upon us, as the Hindu Yoghees proves and teacheth.   And ye see how, by the south-wind, the air is condensed into thin clouds, in which, as in a looking-glass, are reflected representations at a great distance, of castles, mountains, horses, men, and other things, which when the clouds are gone, presently vanish.—And Kunz-Pnjua, in his Meteors, shews that a rainbow is conceived in a cloud of the air, as in a looking-glass.—And the effigies of bodies may, by the strength of Nature, in a moist air, be easily represented; in the same manner as the representations of things are in things.—The author knows of a man, to whom it happened, by reason of the weakness of his sight, that the air that was near him became, as it were, a looking-glass to him, and the optic-beam did reflect back upon himself, and could not penetrate the air, so that, whithersoever he went, he thought he saw his own image, with his face towards him, go before him.—In like manner, by the artificialness of some certain looking-glass, may be produced at a distance, in the air, besides the looking-glasses, what images we please, which, when ignorant men see, they think they see the appearances of spirits or souls—when, indeed, they are nothing else but semblances akin to themselves, and without life. And it is well known, if in a dark place, where there is no light but by the coming in of a beam of the sun somewhere through a little hole, a white paper or plain looking-glass be set up against the light, that there may be seen upon them whatsoever things are done without, being shined upon by the sun. And there is another Magic yet more wonderful:—if any one shall take images, artificially painted, or written letters, and, in a clear night, set them against the beams of the full moon, those resemblances being multiplied in the air, and caught upward, and reflected back together with the beams of the moon, another man, that is privy to the thing, at a long distance, sees, reads, and knows them in the very compass and circle of the moon; which art of declaring secrets is, indeed, very profitable for towns and cities that are besieged, being a thing which Pythagoras long since did, and which is not unknown to some in these days; I will not except myself. And all these things and many more, and much greater than these, are grounded in the very nature of the air, and have their reasons and causes declared in mathematics and optics. And as these resemblances are reflected back to the sight, so also are they, sometimes, to the hearing, as is manifest in echo. But there are many more secret arts than these, and such whereby any one may, at a remarkable distance, hear, and understand distinctly, what another speaks or whispers.

The next in order, after the four simple elements, are the four kinds of perfect bodies compounded in them, viz., metals. stones, plants, and animals; and although in the generation of each of these, all the elements combine together in the composition, yet every one of them follows and resembles one of the elements which is most predominant; for all stones, being earthy, are naturally heavy, and are so hardened with dryness that they cannot be melted;—but metals are watery, and may be melted, which naturalists and chemists find to be true, viz., that they are com-

posed or generated of a viscous water, or watery *argent vive.* Plants
have such an affinity with the air, that unless they are out in it, and
receive its benefit, they neither flourish nor increase.   So also animals,
as the Poet finally expresses it—

"Have, in their natures, a most fiery force,
"And also spring from a celestial source:"

and fire is so natural to them that, being extinguished, they soon die.

Now, amongst stones, those that are dark and heavy, are called
earthy—those which are transparent, of the *watery element,* as crystal,
beryl, and pearls—those which swim upon the water and are spongious,
as the pumice-stone, sponge, and sophus, are called airy—and those are
attributed to the element of fire, out of which fire is extracted, or which
are resolved into fire; as thunder-stones, fire-stones, asbestos.   Also,
amongst metals; lead and silver are earthy; quicksilver is watery; copper
and tin, airy; gold and iron, fiery.   In plants, also, the roots resemble
earth—the leaves, water—flowers, the air—and seed, the fire, by reason
of their multiplying spirit.   Besides, some are hot, some cold, some
moist, others dry, borrowing their names from the qualities of the elements.   Amongst animals, also, some are, in comparison of others,
earthy, because they live in the very bowels of the earth, as worms,
moles, and many other reptiles; others watery, as fish; others which
always abide in the air, therefore airy; others, again, fiery, as sala-
manders, crickets; and such as are of a fiery heat, as pigeons, ostriches,
eagles, lions, panthers, &c., &c.

Now, in animals, the bones resemble earth—vital spirit, the fire—
flesh, the air—and humors, the water; and these humors also resemble
the elements, viz., yellow choler, the fire—the blood, the air—phlegm,
the water—and black choler, or melancholy, the earth.   And, lastly, in
the soul itself, the understanding resembles the fire—reason, the air—
imagination, the water—and the senses the earth.   And these senses
again are divided amongst themselves, according to the elements; for
the sight is fiery, because it cannot perceive without the help of fire and
light—the hearing is airy, for a sound is made by the striking of the air
—the smell and taste resemble water, without the moisture of which
there is neither smell nor taste—and, lastly, the feeling is wholly earthly,
because it takes gross bodies for its object.   The actions, also, and operations of man are governed by the elements: for the earth signifies a
slow and firm motion; the water, fearfulness, sluggishness, and remiss-
ness in working; air signifies cheerfulness, and an amiable disposition;
but fire, a fierce, working, quick, susceptible disposition.   The elements
are, therefore, the first and original matter of all things; and all things
are of and according to them; and they in and through all things diffuse
their virtues.

In the original and exemplary world, all things are all in all; so also in this corporeal world. And the elements are not only in these inferior things, but in all things.

Now it must be understood that in these inferior bodies the elements are gross and corruptible; but in the heavens they are, with their natures and virtues, after a celestial and more excellent manner than in sublunary things; for the firmness of the celestial earth is there without the grossness of water; and the agility of air without exceeding its bounds; the heat of fire without burning, only shining, giving light and life to all things by its celestial heat.—Now amongst the stars, or planets, some are fiery, as Mars, and the Sun—airy, as Jupiter, and Venus—watery, as Saturn, and Mercury—and earthy, such as inhabit the eighth orb, and the Moon (which by many is accounted watery), seeing that, as if it were earth, it attracts to itself the celestial waters, with which being imbibed, it does, on account of its proximity to us, pour forth and communicate to our globe.

There are, likewise, among the signs, some fiery, some airy, some watery, and some earthy. The elements rule *them,* also, in the heavens, distributing to them these four threefold considerations of every element, according to their triplicities, viz., the beginning, middle, and end.

Likewise, devils are distinguished according to the elements; for some are called earthy devils, others fiery, some airy, and others watery. Hence, also, those four infernal rivers: fiery Phlegethon, airy Cocytus, watery Styx, earthy Acheron. Also, in the Gospel, we read of comparisons of the elements: as hell fire, and eternal fire, into which the cursed shall be commanded to go;—and in Revelations, of a lake of fire: —and Isaiah, speaking of the damned, says that the Lord will smite them with corrupt air;—and in Job, they shall skip from the waters of the snow to the extremity of heat; and, in the same, we read, that the earth is dark, and covered with the darkness of death, and *miserable* darkness.

And these elements are placed in the high spirits, and the blessed intelligences: there is in them a stability of their essence, which is an earthy virtue. By the Psalmist they are called waters, where he says— "Who rulest the waters that are higher than the heavens;"—also, in them their subtle breath is air, and their love is shining fire; hence they are called in Scripture, the wings of the wind; and, in another place, the Psalmist speaks of them thus—"Who makest angels thy spirits, and thy ministers, a flaming fire!"—Also, according to the different orders of spirits or angels, some are fiery, as seraphims, authorities, and powers— earthy, as cherubim—watery, as thrones and archangels—airy, as dominions and principalities.

And do we not read of the original Maker of all things, that the earth shall be opened and bring forth a Saviour?—Likewise it is spoken of the same, that he shall be a fountain of living water, cleansing and regenerating; and the same spirit breathing the breath of life; and the same, according to Moses' and Paul's testimony—*a consuming fire.*

That the elements are, therefore, to be found everywhere, and in all things, after their manner, no man will dare to deny: first, in these inferior bodies, feculent and gross; and in celestials, more pure and clear; but in supercelestials, living and in all respects blessed. Elements, therefore, in the exemplary world, are ideas of things to be produced; in intelligences they are distributed powers; in the heavens, they are virtuous; and in inferior bodies, are gross forms.

It is to be noted, that the Universal Spirit (God), in the first place, is the end and beginning of all virtue; he gives the *seal* of the *ideas* to his servants, *the intelligences,* who, as faithful officers, *sign* all things entrusted to them with an *ideal virtue;* the heavens and stars, as instruments, disposing the matter, in the meanwhile, for the receiving of those forms which reside in Divine Majesty, and to be conveyed by stars. And the Giver of forms distributes them by the ministry of his intelligences, which he has ordained as rulers and controllers over his works; to whom such a power is entrusted, in things committed to them, that so all virtue in stones, herbs, metals, and all other things, may come from the intelligences, the governors. Therefore the form and virtue of things come first from the *ideas*—then from the ruling and governing intelligences—then from the aspects of the stars disposing—and, lastly, from the tempers of the elements disposed, answering the influences of the heavens, by which the elements themselves are ordered or disposed. These kinds of operations, therefore, are performed in these inferior things by express forms; and in the heavens, by disposing virtues; in intelligences, by mediating rules; in the original cause, by *ideas* and exemplary forms; all of which must of necessity agree in the execution of the effect and virtue of everything.

There is, therefore, a wonderful virtue and operation in every herb and stone, but greater in a star; beyond which, even from the governing intelligences, everything receives and obtains many things for itself, especially from the Supreme Cause, with whom all things mutually and exactly correspond, agreeing in a harmonious consent.

Therefore there is *no other cause* of the necessity of effects, than the connection of all things with the First Cause and their correspondency with those divine patterns and eternal ideas, whence everything hath its determinate and particular place in the exemplary world, from whence it lives and receives its original being; and every virtue of herbs, stones, metals, animals, words, speeches, and all things that are of God, are placed there.

Now the First Cause, The GREAT UNIVERSAL SPIRIT (which is God), although he doth, by intelligences and the heavens, work upon these inferior things, does sometimes (these mediums being laid aside, or their officiating being suspended) work those things immediately by himself—which works are then called miracles. But whereas secondary causes do, by the command and appointment of the First Cause, necessarily act, and are necessitated to produce their effects if God (the First Cause) shall, notwithstanding, according to his pleasure, so discharge and suspend them that they shall wholly desist from the necessity of that command, then they are called the greatest miracles of Divine Wisdom (God). For instance: the fire of the *Chaldean* furnace did not burn the children; the sun stood still at the command of *Joshua* and became retrograde one whole day; also, at the prayer of *Hezekiah*, it went back ten degrees; and when our *Saviour Christ* was crucified, it became darkened, though at full moon.

And the reason of these operations can by no rational discourse, no Magic or science, Occult or profound soever, be found out or understood; but are to be learned by Divine oracles only.*

Now seeing that the soul is the essential form, intelligible and incorruptible, and is the first mover of the body, and is moved of itself; but that the body, or matter, is of itself unable and unfit for motion, and does very much degenerate from the soul, it appears that there is need of a more excellent medium: now such a medium is conceived to be the spirit of the world, or that which some call a quintessence; because it is not from the four elements, but a certain *first thing,* having its being above and beside them. There is, therefore, such a kind of medium required to be, by which celestial souls may be joined to gross bodies, and bestow upon them wonderful gifts. This spirit is, in the same manner, in the body of the world, as our spirit is in our bodies; for as the powers of our soul are communicated to the members of the body by the medium of the spirit, so also the virtue of the soul of the world is diffused, throughout all things, by the medium of the universal spirit; for there is nothing to be found in the whole world that hath not a spark of the virtue thereof. Now this spirit is received into things, more or less, by the rays of the stars, so far as things are disposed, or made fit recipients of it. By this spirit, therefore, every occult property is conveyed into herbs, stones, metals, and animals, through the sun, moon, planets, and through stars higher than the planets. Now this spirit may be more advantageous to us if we knew how to separate it from the elements; or, at least, to use those things chiefly which are most abounding with this spirit. For those things in which the spirit is less drowned in a body, and less checked by matter, do much more powerfully and perfectly act, and also more readily generate their like; for in it are all

---

* The foregoing Chapter, if well considered, will open the intellect to a more easy comprehension of the Magical Science of Nature, etc.; and will facilitate, in a wonderful degree, thy studies in these sublime mysteries.

generative and *seminal virtues*. For which cause the alchymist endeavors to separate this spirit from gold and silver, which, being rightly separated and extracted, if it shall be afterwards projected upon any metal, turns it into gold or silver; which is in no way impossible or improbable, when we consider that by art that may be done in a short time, what Nature, in the bowels of the earth (as in a matrix), perfects in a very long space of time.

All stars have their peculiar natures, properties, and conditions, the seals and characters whereof they produce through their rays even in these inferior things, viz., in elements, in stones, in plants, in animals, and their members; whence every thing receives from an harmonious disposition, and from its star shining upon it, some particular seal or character stamped upon it, which is the significator of that star or harmony, containing in it a peculiar virtue; different from other virtues of the same matter, both generically, specifically, and numerically. Every thing, therefore, hath its *character* impressed upon it by its *star* for some peculiar effect, especially by that star which doth principally govern it; and these characters contain in them the particular natures, virtues, and roots of their stars, and produce the like operations upon other things on which they are reflected; and stir up and help the influence of their stars, whether they be planets, or fixed stars and figures, or celestial constellations, viz., as often as they shall be made in a fit matter, and in their due and accustomed times; which the ancient wise men (considering such as labored much in finding out occult properties of things) did set down, in writing, the images of the stars, their figures, seals, marks, characters, such as Nature herself did describe by the rays of the stars in these inferior bodies: some in stones, some in plants, some in joints and knots of trees and their boughs, and some in various members of animals. For the bay-tree, lote-tree, and marigold, are solary herbs, and their roots and knots being cut, they show the characters of the sun; and in stones the character and images of celestial things are often found. But there being so great a diversity of things, there is only a traditional knowledge of a few things which human understanding is able to reach; therefore very few of those things are known to us, which the ancient philosophers and chiromancers attained to, partly by reason and partly by experience; and there yet lie hid many things in the treasury of Nature, which the diligent student and wise searcher shall contemplate and discover.

THE EFFICACY AND VIRTUE OF PERFUMES.

Efficacy of Perfumes. It is necessary, before I come to the operative or practical part of Talismanic Magic, to show the compositions of fumes or vapors, that are proper to the stars, and are of great force for

the opportunely receiving of celestial gifts, under the rays of the stars—
inasmuch as they strongly work upon the air and breath; for our breath
is very much changed by such kind of vapors, if both vapors be of the
other like.   The air being also, through the said vapors, easily moved,
or infected with the qualities of inferiors, or celestial (daily quickly
penetrating our breast and vitals), does wonderfully reduce us to the
like qualities.   Let no man wonder how great things suffumigations can
do in the air; especially when they shall, know that the Master Lamas,
by certain vapors exhaled from proper suffumigations, æerial spirits are
raised; also thunder and lightnings, and the like: as the liver of a
cameleon being burnt on the house top, will raise showers and lightnings;
the same effect has the head and throat, if they are burnt with oaken
wood.   There are some suffumigations under the influences of the stars,
that cause images of spirits to appear in the air, or elsewhere; for if
Temple Incense be made to fume, by invocations spirits should soon
come together, being attracted by the vapors which are most congruous to their own natures;   hence, Temple Incense is called the
herbs of the spirits.   Also I saith, that if a fume be made of the root
of the reedy herb sagapen, with the juice of hemlock and henbane, and
the herb tapsus barbatus, red sanders, and black poppy, it will likewise
make strange shapes appear; but if a suffume be made of smallage, it
chases them away, and destroys their visions.   Again, if a perfume is
made of calamint, piony, mint, and palma christi, it drives away all evil
spirits and vain imaginations.   Likewise, by certain fumes, animals are
gathered together, and put to flight.   Concerning the stone liparis, that,
with the fume, thereof, all beasts are attracted together.   The bones in
the upper part of the throat of a hart, being burnt, bring serpents together; but the horn of the hart, being burnt, chases away the same;
likewise, a fume of peacock's feathers does the same.   Also, the lungs
of an ass, being burnt, puts all poisonous things to flight; and the fume
of the burnt hoof of a horse drives away mice; the same does the hoof
of a mule; and with the hoof of the left-foot flies are driven away.   And
if a house, or any place, be smoked with the *gall* of a *cuttle-fish* made
into a confection with red storax, roses, and lignum aloes, and then there
be some sea-water or blood cast into that place, the whole house will
seem to be full of water or blood.

Now such kind of vapors as these, we must conceive, do infect a
body, and infuse a virtue into it which continues long, even as the
poisonous vapor of the pestilence, being kept for two years in the walls
of a house, infects the inhabitants; and as the contagion of pest or
leprosy lying hid in a garment, will, long after, infect him that wears it.

Now there are certain suffumigations made from Temple Incense
and used by almost all The High-Grade Adepts.   For if any one shall
hide gold, or silver, or any other such like precious thing (the moon being

in conjunction with the sun), and shall perfume the place with Temple Incense, that thing which is so hid shall never be taken away therefrom, but that spirits shall continually keep it; and if any one shall endeavor to take it away by force, they shall be hurt, or struck with a frenzy. And there is nothing like fume of spermaceti for the raising up of spirits; therefore if a fume be made of that, lignum aloes, pepperwort, musk, saffron, and red storax, tempered together with the blood of a lapwing or bat, it will quickly gather airy spirits to the place where it is used; and if it be used above the graves of the dead, it will attract spirits and ghosts thither.

Now the use of suffumigation is this: that whenever you set about making any talisman, image, or the like, under the rule of dominion of any star or planet, you should by no means omit the making of a suffumigation appropriate to that planet or constellation under which you desire to work any effect or wonderful operation; as for instance:— when I direct any work to the sun, I must suffume with solary things; if to the moon, with lunary things; and so of the rest. And I must be careful to observe that as there is a contrariety, or antipathy, in the natures of the stars and planets and their spirits, so there is also in suffumigations: for there is an antipathy between lignum, aloes and sulphur, frankincense and quicksilver; and spirits that are raised by the fume of lignum aloes, are laid by the burning of sulphur. For the learned Hindus gives an example of a spirit that appeared in the form of a lion, furious and raging: by setting a white cock before the apparition it soon vanished away; because there is so great a contrariety between a cock and a lion;—and let this suffice for a general observation in these kind of things. I shall proceed with showing distinctly the composition of the several fumes appropriated to the seven planets.

COMPOSITION OF PERFUMES APPROPRIATED TO THE SEVEN PLANETS.

THE SUN. ☉

I make a suffumigation for the sun in this manner:—

Take of saffron, ambergeris, musk, lignum aloes, lignum balsam, the fruit of the laurel, cloves, myrrh, and frankincense; of each a like quantity; all of which being bruised and mixed together, so as to make a sweet odor, must be incorporated with the brain of an eagle, or the blood of a white cock, after the manner of pills, or troches.

THE MOON. ☽

For the moon, I make a suffume of the head of a frog dried, and the eyes of a bull, the seed of white poppies, frankincense, and camphire, which must be incorporated with menstruous blood, or the blood of a goose.

SATURN. ♄

For saturn take the seed of black poppies, henbane, mandrake root, load-stone, and myrrh, and mix them up with the brain of a cat and the blood of a bat.

JUPITER. ♃

Take the seed of ash, lignum aloes, storax, the gum Benjamin, the lapis lazuli, the tops of peacocks' feathers, and incorporate with the blood of a stork, or swallow, or the brain of a hart.

MARS. ♂

Take uphorbium, bdellium, gum armoniac, the roots of both hellebores, the loadstone, and a little sulphur, and incorporate them altogether with the brain of a hart, the blood of a man, and the blood of a black cat.

VENUS. ♀

Take musk, ambergris, lignum aloes, red roses, and red coral, and make them up with sparrow's brains and pigeon's blood.

MERCURY. ☿

Take mastich, frankincense, cloves, and the herb cinquefoil, and the agate stone, and incorporate them all with the brain of a fox, or weasel, and the blood of a magpie.

GENERAL FUMES OF THE PLANETS.

To Saturn are appropriated for fumes, odoriferous roots: as pepperwort root, &c., and the frankincense tree. To *Jupiter,* all odoriferous fruits: as nutmegs, cloves, &c. To *Mars,* all odoriferous woods: as sanders, cyprus, lignum balsam, and lignum aloes. To the *Sun,* all gums: as frankincense, mastich benjamin, storax, laudanum, ambergris, and musk. To *Venus,* flowers: as roses, violets, saffron, and the like. To Mercury, all the parings of wood or fruit: as cinnamon, lignum cassia, mace, citron peel, and bayberries, and whatever seeds are odoriferous. To the Moon, the leaves of all vegetables: as the leaf indum, the leaf of the myrtle, and bay tree. Know, also, that according to the opinion of all magicians, in every good matter (as love, good-will, &c.), there must be a good perfume, odoriferous and precious;—and in evil matters (as hatred, anger, misery, and the like), there must be a stinking fume that is of no worth.

The twelve Signs of the Zodiac also have their proper suffumigations, viz., Aries, *myrrh;* Taurus, *pepper-wort;* Gemini, *mastich;* Cancer, *camphire;* Leo, *frankincense;* Virgo, *sanders;* Libra, *galbanum;* Scorpio, *oppoponax;* Sagittarius, *ignum aloes;* Capricorn, *benjamin;* Aquarius, *euphorbium;* Pisces, *red storax.* But I describe the most powerful fume to be, that which is compounded of the seven aromatics, according to the powers of the seven planets; for it receives from *Saturn,* pepper-wort; from *Jupiter,* nutmeg; from *Mars,* lignum aloes; from the *Sun,* mastich; from *Venus,* saffron; from *Mercury,* cinnamon; and from the *Moon,* myrtle.

By a close observation of the above order of suffumigations, conjoined with other things of which I shall speak hereafter (necessary to the full accomplishment of Talismanic Magic), many wonderful effects may be caused especially if I keep in eye what was delivered in the first part of my Magic, viz., that the soul of the operator must go along with this: otherwise, in vain is *suffumigation, seal, ring, image, picture, glass,* or any other instrument of magic: seeing that it is not merely the disposition, but the act of the disposition, and firm and powerful intent or imagination that gives the effect.—I shall now hasten to speak, generally, of the construction of rings magical, and their wonderful and potent virtues and operations.

Magic Rings. Rings, when they are opportunely made, impress their virtues upon us insomuch that they affect the spirit of him that carries them with gladness or sadness; and render him bold or fearful, courteous or terrible, amiable or hateful; inasmuch, also as they fortify us against sickness, poisons, enemies, evil spirits, and all manner of hurtful things; and often, where the law has no effect, these little trifles greatly assist and corroborate the troubled spirit of the wearer, and help him, in a wonderful manner, to overcome his adversaries, while they do wonder how it is that they cannot effect any hurtful undertaking against him. These things, I say, are great helps against wrathful, vicious, worldly-minded men, inasmuch as they do terrify, hurt, and render invalid the machinations of those who would otherwise work our misery or destruction. All of which we are neither afraid nor ashamed to declare, well knowing that these things will be hid from the wicked and profane, so as that they cannot draw the same into any abuse, or privy mischief toward their neighbor; we having reserved some few things in this art to ourselves—not wishing to throw pearls before swine. And however simple and plain we may describe some certain experiments and operations (so as that the great-mouthed school philosophers may mutter or scoff thereat), yet there is nothing delivered in this book but what may be, by an understanding thereof, brought into effect, and, likewise, out of which some good may be derived. But to proceed.

The manner of making of these rings is thus:—when any star ascends in the horoscope (fortunately), with a fortunate aspect or conjunction of the moon, we proceed to take a *stone* and herb, that is under that star, and likewise make a ring of the metal that is corresponding to the star; and in the ring, under the stone, put the herb or root, not forgetting to inscribe the *effect, image, name* and *character,* as also the proper suffume. But I shall speak more of these in another place, where I speak of images and characters. Therefore, in making of rings magical, these things are unerringly to be observed as we have ordered;—if any one is willing to work any effect or experiment in Magic, he must by no means neglect the necessary circumstances which we have so uniformly delivered. A Prince of the Indians bestowed seven rings, marked with the virtues and names of the seven planets, to *Appollonius,* of which he wore one every day, distinguishing according to the names of the days; by the benefit of which he lived above one hundred and thirty years, as also always retained the beauty of his youth. In like manner, Moses, the Lawgiver and Ruler of the Hebrews, being skilled in the Egyptian Magic, is said, by Josephus, to have made rings of love and oblivion. There was also, teacheth the Hindu Adepts, a ring of Battas, which could procure love and honor. We read, also, that Eudamus, a certain philosopher, made rings against the bites of serpents, bewitchings and evil spirits. The same doth Josephus relate of Solomon. Also we read, in Plato, that *Gygus, King of Lydia,* had a ring of wonderful and strange virtues; the seal of which, when he turned it toward the palm of his hand, no body could see him, but he could see all things; by the opportunity of which ring he ravished the Queen and slew the King his master, and killed whomsoever he thought stood in his way; and in these villanies nobody could see him; and at length, by the benefit of this ring, he became *King of Lydia.**

THE CELESTIAL POWERS OF THE SOUL.

Soul. The Powers of the Soul are much helped, and are helpful, and become most powerful, by virtue of Astral Spirits, as they agree with the spirits—either by any natural agreement, or voluntary election; for, as the Adepts teach, he who chuseth that which is the better, seems to differ nothing from him who hath this of Nature. It conduceth, therefore, very much for the receiving the benefit of the spirits, in any work, if we shall, by the spirits, make ourselves suitable to them in our thoughts, affections, imaginations, elections, deliberations, contemplations, and the like. For such like passions vehemently stir up our spirit to their likeness, and suddenly expose us, and our's, to the superior significators of

---

* I have above shewn the power and virtue of Magical rings; but the particular characters, inscriptions, and images to be made in, or upon them, I refer the student to that chapter treating of "The Composition of various Talismans"; in which I have described exactly the express methods of perfecting them.

such like passions; and also, by reason of their dignity and nearness to the superiors, do partake more of the celestials than any material things; for our mind can, through imaginations or reason by a kind of imitation, be so conformed to any spirits, as suddenly to be filled with the virtues of that spirit, as if we were a proper receptacle of the influence thereof. Now the contemplating mind, as it withdraws itself from all *sense, imagination, nature,* and *deliberation,* and calls itself back to things separated, effects divers things by faith, which is a firm adhesion, a fixed intention, and vehement application of the worker or receiver to him that co-operates in any thing, and gives power to the work which we intend to do. So that there is made, as it were, in us the image of the virtue to be received, and the thing to be done in us, or by us. We must, therefore, in every work and application of things, *affect vehemently,* imagine, hope, and believe strongly, for that will be a great help. And it is verified amongst physicians, that a strong belief, and an undoubted hope, and love towards the physician, conduce much to health, yea more sometimes than the medicine itself; for the same that the efficacy and virtue of the medicine works, the same doth the strong imagination of the physician work, being able to change the qualities of the body of the sick, especially when the patient places much confidence in the physician, by that means disposing himself for the receiving the virtue of the physician, and physic. *Therefore, he that works in Art Magic must be of a constant belief, be credulous, and not at all doubt of the obtaining of the effect, for as a firm and strong belief doth work wonderful things, although it be in false works—so distrust and doubting doth dissipate and break the virtue of the Soul of the worker, which is the medium betwixt both extremes; whence it happens that he is frustrated of the desired influence of the superiors, which could not be enjoined and united to our labours without a firm and solid virtue of our mind.*

The *Hindu philosophers,* especially the *Lamas,* say, that man's mind, when it is most intent upon any work, through its passion and effects, is joined with the mind of the stars and intelligences, and, being so joined, is the cause that some wonderful virtue be infused into our works and things; and this, as because there is in it an apprehension and power of all things, so because all things have a natural obedience to it, and of necessity an efficacy, and more to that which desired them with a strong desire. And according to this is verified the art of characters, images, enchantments, and some speeches, and many other wonderful experiments, to every thing which the mind affects. By this means, whatsoever the mind of him that is in vehement love effects, hath an efficacy to cause love; and whatsoever the mind of him that strongly hates, dictates, hath an efficacy to hurt and destroy. The like is in other things which the mind affects with a strong desire; for all those things which the mind acts, and dictates by *characters, figures, words, speeches, gestures, and the like,* help the appetite of the soul, and acquire certain wonderful virtues, from the soul of the operator, in that hour when such a like appetite doth invade it; so from the opportunity and celestial influence, moving the mind in this or that manner: for our mind, when it is carried upon the great excess of any passion or virtue, oftentimes takes to itself a strong, better, and more convenient hour or opportunity; which Thomas Aquinas, in his third book against the Gentiles, allows. So, many wonderful virtues both cause and follow certain admirable operations by great affections, in those things which the soul doth dictate in that hour to them. But know, that such kind of things confer nothing, or very little, but to the author of them, and to him who is inclined to them, as if he were the author of them; and this is the manner by which their efficacy is found out. And it is a general rule in them, that every mind, that is more excellent in its desire and affection, makes such like things more fit for itself, as also efficacious to that which it desires. Every one, therefore, that is willing to work in Magic, must know the *virtue, measure, order,* and degree of his own soul in the power of the universe.

THE EFFICACY OF NUMBERS IN THE CONSTRUCTION OF TALISMANS.

Efficacy of Numbers. The doctrines of mathematics are so necessary to and have such an affinity with Magic, that they who profess it without them are quite out of the way, and labor in vain, and shall in no wise obtain their desired effect. For whatsoever things are, and are done in these inferior natural virtues, are all done and governed by *number, weight, measure, harmony, motion* and *light:* and all things which we see in these inferiors have root and foundation in them; yet, nevertheless, without natural virtues of mathematical doctrines, only works like to naturals can be produced: as Adepts teach—a thing not partaking of truth or divinity, but certain images akin to them (as bodies going, or speaking, which yet want the animal faculty), such as were those which, amongst the ancients, were called *Dedalus'* images, and αντοματα, of which *Rajupa-Kin* makes mention, viz., the three-footed images of Vulcan and Dedalus moving themselves; which, *Bunki* saith, came out of their own accord to the exercise; and which, we read, moved themselves at the feast of *Hiarba,* the philosophical exerciser. So there are made glasses (some concave, others of the form of a column) making the representation of things in the air seem like shadows at a distance; of which sort Vivikuzui and Muzebjoia in their books, "Zu-Szekunbuza" and "*Zpeculis,*" taught the making and the use. And we read that *Zunkin Knijuzzi* brought a certain glass, amongst the spoils from the

North of India, in which were seen armies of armed men. And there are made certain transparent glasses, which (being dipped in some certain juices of herbs, and irradiated with an artificial light), fill the whole air round about with visions. And I know how to make reciprocal glasses, in which the sun shining, all things which were illustrated by the rays thereof are apparently seen many miles off. Hence an Adept (expert in natural philosophy and mathematics, and knowing the middle sciences, consisting of both these, viz., arithmetic., music, geometry, optics, astronomy, and such sciences that are of weights, measures, proportions, articles and joints; knowing, also, mechanical arts resulting from these) may, without any wonder, if he excel other men in the art and wit, do many wonderful things, which men may much admire. There are some relics now extant of the ancients, viz., Hercules and Alexander's pillars; the gate of Caspia, made of brass, and shut with iron beams, that it could by no art be broken; and the pyramids of *Julius Cæsar,* erected at *Rome,* near the hill *Vaticanus;* and mountains built by art in the middle of the sea; and towers, and heaps of stones, such as I have seen in England, put together by incredible art. But the vulgar seeing any wonderful sight, impute it to the Devil as his work; or think it a miracle which, indeed, is a work of natural or mathematical philosophy. But here it is convenient that you know, that, as by natural virtues I collect natural virtues; so by abstracted, mathematical, and celestial, I receive Celestial virtues; as Motion, Sense, Life, Speech, *Soothsaying,* and *Divination* even in matter less disposed, as that which is not made by nature, but only by art. And so images that speak, and foretell things to come, are made: as William of Paris relates of a brazen-head, made under the rising of *Saturn,* which, they say, spake with a man's voice. But he that will chuse a disposed matter, and most fit to receive, and a most powerful agent, shall undoubtedly produce more powerful effects. For it is a general opinion of the *Hindu Adepts,* that, as mathematical are more formal than natural, so also they are more efficacious; as they have less dependence in their being, so also in their operation. But amongst all mathematical things, *numbers,* as they have more of form in them, so also are more efficacious, as well to affect what is good as what is bad. All things, which were first made by the nature of things in its first age, are formed by the proportion of numbers; for this was the principle pattern in the mind of the Creator. Hence is borrowed the number of the elements—hence the courses of times—hence the motion of the stars, and the revolution of the heavens, and the state of all things subsist by the uniting together of numbers. Numbers, therefore, are endowed with great and sublime virtues. For it is no wonder, seeing there are so many Occult virtues in natural things, although of manifest operations, that there should be in numbers much greater and more Occult, and also more wonderful and efficacious; for as much as they are more formal, more perfect, and naturally in the celestials, not mixed with separate substances; and, lastly, having the greatest and most simple commixion with the laws of nature, from which they receive their proper and most efficacious virtues; wherefore they also are of most force, and conduce most to the obtaining of spiritual and divine gifts—as, in natural things, elementary qualities are powerful in the transmuting of any elementary thing. Again, all things that are, and are made, subsist by and receive their virtue from numbers:—for time consists of numbers—and all motion and action, and all things which are subject to time and motion. Harmony, also, and voices have their power by and consist of numbers and their proportions; and the proportion arising from numbers do, by lines and points, make characters and figures; and these are proper to *Magical* operations—the middle, which is betwixt both, being appropriated by declining to the extremes, as in the use of letters. And lastly, all species of natural things, and of those which are above Nature, are joined together by certain numbers; hence the Hindus teach that number is that by which all things subsist, and distributes each virtue to each number. And they teach, number hath always a being: yet there is one in voice—another in proportion of them —another in the soul and reason—and another in divine things. And they do so extol numbers, that they think no man can be a true philosopher without them. By them there is a way made for the searching out and understanding of all things knowable;—by them the next access to natural prophecying is had—and the Master Lama proceeds no other way in his prophecies, but by formal numbers.

That there lies wonderful efficacy and virtue in numbers, as well to good as to bad, the most eminent Hindu Adepts and Master Lamas unanimously teach; this especially *Mohnamkhau, Rajputna, Pooramil, Mabahli, Byra,* and many more conform. Hence *Pooramil,* in his commentaries upon the Ankees, testifies that the seventy elders, according to the efficacy of numbers, brought the *Magi-s* into order. The *natural number* is not here considered; but the *formal* consideration that is in the number;—and let that which I spoke of before always be kept in mind, viz., that these powers are not in vocal numbers of merchants buying and selling; but in rational, formal and natural;—these are the distinct mysteries of the *Hindu Adepts.* But he who knows how to join together the vocal numbers and natural with divine, and order them into the same harmony, shall be able to work and know wonderful things by numbers; in which, unless there was a great mystery, John had not said, in the Revelation—"He that hath understanding, let him compute the number of the name of the beast, which is the number of a man;"—and this is the most famous manner of computing amongst the *Hindus* and *Cabalists,* as I shall shew afterwards. But this you must know, that simple numbers signify divine things, numbers of ten; celestial numbers of an hundred; terrestial numbers of a thousand—those things that shall be in a future age. Besides, seeing the parts of the mind are according to an arithmetical mediocrity, by reason of the identity, or equality of excess, coupled together; but the body, whose parts differ in their greatness, is, according to a geometrical mediocrity, compounded; but an animal consists of both, viz., soul and body, according to that mediocrity which is suitable to harmony. Hence it is that *numbers* work very much upon the *soul, figures* upon the *body,* and *harmony* upon the *whole animal.*

SCALE OF UNITY.

Now let me treat particularly of numbers themselves; and, because number is nothing else but a repetition of unity, let me first consider unity itself; for unity doth most simply go through every number, and

THE SCALE OF UNITY.

In the Exemplary World,	Jod.	One Divine Essence, the fountain of all virtues and power, whose name is expressed with one most simple letter.
In the Intellectual World,	The Soul of the World.	One Supreme Intelligence, the first creature, the fountain of life.
In the Celestial World,	The Sun.	One King of Stars, the fountain of life.
In the Elemental World,	The Philosophers' Stone.	One subject, and instrument of all virtues, natural and supernatural.
In the Lesser World,	The Heart.	One first living and last dying.
In the Infernal World,	Lucifer.	One Prince of Rebellion, of Angels, and Darkness.

is the common measure, fountain, and original of all numbers; contains every number joined together in itself entirely; the beginner of every multitude, always the same, and unchangeable; whence, also, being multiplied into itself, produceth nothing but itself: it is indivisible, void of all parts. Nothing is before one, nothing is after one, and beyond it is nothing; and all things which are, desire that one, because all things proceed from one: and that all things may be the same, it is necessary that they partake of that one: and as all things proceed of one into many things, so all things endeavor to return to that one, from which they proceeded; it is necessary that they should put off multitude. One, therefore, is referred to the Universal Spirit, God, who, seeing he is one and innumerable, yet creates innumerable things of himself, and contains them within himself. There is, therefore, one God—one world of the one God—one sun of the one world—also one phœnix in the world—one king amongst bees—one leader amongst flocks of cattle—one ruler amongst herds of beasts—and cranes follow one, and many other animals honor unity. Amongst the members of the body there is one principal, by which all the rest are guided; whether it be the head, or (as some will) the heart. There is one element, overcoming and penetrating all things, viz., fire. There is one thing created of God, the subject of *all wondering* which is in earth or in heaven—it is actually animal, vegetable, and mineral; every where found, known by few, called by none by its proper name, but covered with figures and riddles, without which neither Alchymy, nor Natural Magic can attain to their complete end or perfection. From the Universal Spirit (God) all men proceeded. The Great Universal Spirit (God) is over all, by all, and in us all. For there is one Father, God, from whence all, and we in him; one Lord Jesus, by whom all, and we by him; one God Holy Ghost, into whom all, and we unto him.

NUMBER TWO AND SCALE.

The first number is two, because it is the first multitude; it can be measured by no number besides unity alone, the common measure of all

THE SCALE OF THE NUMBER TWO.

In the Exemplary World,	יה Jah אל El		The names of God, expressed with two Letters.
In the Intellectual World,	An Angel,	The Soul;	Two Intelligible Substances.
In the Celestial World,	The Sun,	The Moon;	Two great Lights.
In the Elementary World,	The Earth,	The Water;	Two Elements producing a living Soul
In the Lesser World,	The Heart,	The Brain;	Two principal Seats of the Soul.
In the Infernal World,	Beemoth, weeping,	Leviathan, gnashing of teeth;	Two Chiefs of the Devils. Two things Christ threatens to the damned.

numbers; it is not compounded of numbers, but of one unity only; neither is it called a number uncompounded, but more properly not compounded. The number three, is called the first number uncompounded.

But the number two is the first branch of unity, and the first procreation; and it is called the number of sicence, and memory, and of light, and the number of man, who is called another, and the lesser world; it is also called the number of charity, and of mutual love; of marriage, and society: as it is said by the Lord—"Two shall be one flesh."—And Solomon saith, "It is better that two be together than one, for they have a benefit by their mutual society: if one shall fall, he shall be supported by the other. Woe to him that is alone; because, when he falls, he hath not another to help him. And if two sleep together, they shall warm one another; how shall one be hot alone?—And if any prevail against him, two resist him." And it is called the number of wedlock, and sex; for there are two sexes—masculine and feminine. And two doves bring forth two eggs; out of the first of which is hatched the male, out of the second, the female. It is also called the middle, that is capable, that is good and bad, partaking; and the beginning of division, of multitude, and distinction; and signifies matter. This is also, sometimes, the number of discord, of confusion, of misfortune and uncleanness; whence St. Hierom, against Jovianus, saith—"that therefore it was not spoken in the second day of the creation of the world.—"And God (spirit) said, that it was good;"—because the number of two is evil. Hence also, it was, that God commanded that all unclean animals should go into the ark by couples; because, as I said, the number of two is a number of uncleanness. *Ytahzmji,* a great *Master Lama,* said, that unity was God. and a good intellect; but that duality was a devil, **and an evil intellect,** in which is a material multitude: wherefore Hindu Adepts say, that two is not a number, but a certain confusion of unities. And Kunjuxz teaches, that the Ytahzmji called unity, Omijun; and two, strife and boldness; and three, justice, which is the highest perfection, and is not without many mysteries. Hence there were two tables of the law in Sinai—two cherubims looking to the propitiatory in *Moses*—two olives dropping oil, in *Zacharia*—two natures in Christ, divine and human: hence Moses saw two appearances of God Spirit,—also two Testaments —two commands of love—two first dignities—two first people—two kinds of spirits, good and bad—two intellectual creatures, an angel and soul—two great lights—two solstitia—two equinoctials—two poles— two elements, producing a living soul, viz., earth and water.

NUMBER THREE AND SCALE.

The number Three, is an uncompounded number, a holy number, a number of perfection, a most powerful number:—for there are three persons in God; there are three theological virtues in religion. Hence it is that this number conduceth to the ceremonies of God and religion, that by the solemnity of which, prayers and sacrifices are thrice repeated; for corporeal and spiritual things consist of three things, viz., beginning, middle, and end. By three, as Ytahzinjiumi saith, the world is perfected—harmony, necessity, and order, *i. e.*, concurrence of causes (which many call fate), and the execution of them to the fruit, or increase, or a due distribution of the increase. The whole measure of time is concluded in three, viz., past, present, and to come; all magnitude is contained in three—line, superfices, and body;—every body consists of three intervals,—length, breadth, and thickness. Harmony contains three consents in time—diapason, hemiolion, diatesseron. There are also three

THE SCALE OF THE NUMBER THREE.

In the Original World,	The Father,	Adai, The Son,	The Holy Ghost;	The name of God with three Letters.
In the Intellectual World,	Supreme Innocents,	Middle Martyrs,	Lowest of all Confessors,	Three hierarchies of Angels. Three degrees of the Blessed.
In the Celestial World,	Moveable Corners, Of the Day,	Fixed, Succeeding, Nocturnal,	Common, Falling; Partaking;	Three quaternions of Signs. Three quaternions of houses. Three Lords of triplicities.
In the Elementary World,	Simple,	Compounded.	Thrice compounded;	Three degrees of elements.
In the Lesser World,	The head, in which the intellect grows, answering to the intellectual world,	The breast, where is the heart, the seat of life, answering to the celestial world,	The belly, where the faculty of generation is, and the genital members, answering the elemental world;	Three parts, answering to the threefold world.
In the Infernal World,	Alecto, Minos, Wicked,	Megera, Acacus, Apostates,	Ctesiphone, Rhadamantus; Infidels;	Three infernal Furies. Three infernal Judges. Three degrees of the damned

kinds of souls—vegetative, sensitive, and intellectual. And as such, saith the Prophet, God (Divine Wisdom), orders the world by number, weight and measure; and the number three is deputed to the ideal forms thereof, as the number two is the procreating matter, and unity to God the maker of it.—Magicians do constitute three Princes of the world.—*Oromasis, Mithris, Araminis; i. e.,* God, the mind, and the spirit. By the three-square or solid, the three numbers of nine, of things produced, are distributed, viz., of the supercelestial into nine orders of intelligences; of celestial, into nine orbs; of inferiors, into nine kinds of generable and corruptible things. Lastly, into this eternal orb, viz., twenty-seven, all musical proportions are included, as *Nukba* and *Tyxuna* do at large discourse; and the number three hath, in a harmony of five, the grace of the first voice. Also, in intelligences, there are three hierarchies of angelical spirits. There are three powers of intellectual creatures— memory, mind, and will. There are three orders of the blessed, viz., martyrs, confessors, and innocents. There are three quaternions of celestial signs, viz., of fixed, movable and common; as also of houses, viz., centres, succeeding and falling. There are, also three faces and heads in every sign, and three Lords of each triplicity. There are three fortunes amongst the planets. In the infernal crew, three judges, three furies, three-headed *Cerberus:* we read, also, of a thrice-double Hecate. Three months of the *Virgin Diana.* Three persons in the supersubstantial Divinity. Three times—of nature, law, and grace. Three theological virtues—faith, hope, and charity. Jonah was three days in the whale's belly; and so many was Christ in the grave.

NUMBER FOUR AND SCALE.

The Adepts call the number Four, Chaitya, and prefer it before all the virtues of numbers, because it is the foundation and root of all other numbers; whence, also, all foundations, as well in artificial things, as natural and divine, are four square, as I shall shew afterwards; and it signifies solidity, which also is demonstrated by a four-square figure; for the number four, is the first four-square plane, which consists of two proportions, whereof the first is of one to two, the latter of two to four; and it proceeds by a double procession and proportion, viz., of one to one, and of two to two—beginning at a unity, and ending at a quaternity: which proportions differ in this, that, according to Arithmetic, they are unequal to one another, but according to Geometry, are equal. Therefore, a four-square is ascribed to God the Father; and also contains the mystery of the whole Trinity: for by its single proportion, viz., by the first of one to one, the unity of the paternal substance is signified, from which proceeds one Son, equal to him; by the next procession, also simple, viz., of two to two, is signified (by the second procession) the Holy Ghost; from both—that the Son be equal to the Father, by the first procession; and the Holy Ghost be equal to both, by the second procession. Hence, that super-excellent and great name of the Divine Trinity in God is written with four letters, viz., *Jod, He,* and *Vau.* He, where it is not the aspiration He, signifies the proceeding of the Spirit from both; for He, being duplicated, terminates both syllables, and the whole name, but is pronounced Jova, as some will whence that Jove of the heathen, which the ancients did picture with four ears; whence the number four, is the fountain and head of the whole, Divinity. And the Hindu Adepts call it the perpetual fountain of Nature: for there are four degrees in the scale of Nature, viz., *to be, to live, to be sensible, to understand.* There are four motions in Nature, viz., ascendant, descendant, going forward, circular. There are four corners in Heaven, viz., rising, falling, the middle of the Heaven, the

THE SCALE OF THE NUMBER FOUR.

The name of God with four letters,	יהוה				In the original world, whence the law of Providence.
Four triplicities, or intelligible hierarchies,	Seraphim, Cherubim, Thrones,	Dominations, Powers, Virtues,	Principalities, Archangels, Angels,	Innocents, Martyrs, Confessors,	In the intellectual world, whence the fatal law.
Four angels ruling over the four corners of the world,	מיכאל Michael,	רפאל Raphael,	נבריאל Gabriel,	איריאל Uriel,	
Four rulers of the elements,	שרפ Seraph,	כרוב Cherub,	תרשיט Tharsis,	אריאל Ariel,	
Four consecrated animals,	The Lion,	The Eagle,	Man,	A Calf,	
Four triplicities of the tribes of Israel,	Dan, Asser, Naphthalin,	Jehuda, Isachar, Zebulun,	Manasse, Benjamin, Ephraim,	Reuben, Simeon, Gad,	
Four triplicities of the Apostles,	Matthias, Peter, Jacob the elder	Simon, Bartholomew, Matthew,	John, Philip, James the Younger,	Thaddeus, Andrew, Thomas,	
Four Evangelists,	Mark,	John,	Matthew,	Luke,	
Four triplicities of signs,	Aries, Leo, Sagittarius,	Gemini, Libra, Aquarius,	Cancer, Scorpion, Pisces,	Taurus, Virgo, Capricornus.	In the celestial world, where the law of Nature.
The stars and planets related to the elements,	Mars, and the Sun,	Jupiter, and Venus,	Saturn, and Mercury,	The fixed Stars, and the Moon.	
Four qualities of the celestial elements,	Light,	Diaphanousness.	Agility,	Solidity.	
Four elements,	אש Fire,	ריח Air,	כוים Water,	עפר Earth.	In the elementary, where the law of generation and corruption is.
Four qualities,	Heat,	Moisture,	Cold,	Dryness.	
Four seasons,	Summer.	Spring,	Winter,	Autumn.	
Four corners of the world,	East,	West,	North,	South.	
Four perfect kinds of mixed bodies,	Animals,	Plants,	Metals,	Stones.	
Four kinds of animals,	Walking,	Flying,	Swimming,	Creeping.	

bottom of it. There are four elements under Heaven, viz., fire, air, water, and earth; according to these there are four triplicities in Heaven. There are four first qualities under Heaven, viz., cold, heat, dryness and moisture; from these are the four humours—blood, phlegm, choler, melancholy. Also, the year is divided into four parts, which are the spring, summer, autumn, and winter:—also the wind is divided into eastern, western, northern, and southern. There are, also, four rivers in Paradise; and so many infernal. Also, the number four makes up all knowledge: first, it fills up every simple progress of numbers with

THE SCALE OF THE NUMBER FOUR.

What answers the elements in plants,	Seeds,	Flowers,	Leaves,	Roots,	
What in metals,	Gold and iron,	Copper and tin,	Quicksilver,	Lead and silver.	
What in stones,	Bright and burning,	Light and transparent,	Clear and congealed,	Heavy and dark.	
Four elements of man,	The Mind,	Spirit,	Soul,	Body.,	In the lesser world, viz. man, from whom is the law of prudence.
Four powers of the soul,	The Intellect,	Reason,	Phantasy,	Sense.	
Four judiciary powers,	Faith,	Science,	Opinion,	Experience.	
Four moral virtues	Justice,	Temperance,	Prudence,	Fortitude.	
The senses answering to the elements,	Sight,	Hearing,	Taste and smell,	Touch.	
Four elements of man's body,	Spirit,	Flesh,	Humours,	Bones.	
A fourfold spirit;	Animal,	Vital,	Generative;	Natural.	
Four humours,	Choler,	Blood,	Phlegm,.	Melancholy.	
Four manners of complexion,	Violence,	Nimbleness,	Dulness,	Slowness.	
Four princes of devils, offensive in the elements,	סמאל Samael,	עזאזל Azazel,	עזאל Azael,	מהזאל Mahazael.	In the infernal world, where is the law of wrath and punishment.
Four infernal rivers,	Phlegethon,	Cocytus,·	Styx,	Acheron.	
Four princes of spirits, upon the four angels of the world,	Oriens,	Paymon,	Egyn,	Amaymon.	

four terms, viz., with one, two, three, and four, constituting the number ten. It fills up every difference of numbers: the first even, and containing the first odd in it. It hath in music, diatesseron—the grace of the fourth voice; also it contains the instrument of four strings; and a Pythagorian diagram, whereby are found out first of all musical tunes, and all harmony of music: for double, treble, four times double, one and a half, one and a third part, a concord of all, a double concord of all, of five, of four, and all consonancy is limited within the bounds of the number four. It doth also contain the whole of Mathematics in four terms, viz., *point, line, superfices,* and *profundity.* It comprehends all Nature in four terms, viz., substance, quality, quantity, and motion; also all natural philosophy, in which are the seminary virtues of Nature, the natural springing the growing form, and the *compositum.* Also metaphysics is comprehended in four bounds, viz., *being, essence, virtue,* and *action.* Moral philosophy is comprehended with four virtues, viz., *prudence, justice, fortitude,* and *temperance.* It hath also the power of justice: hence, a four-fold law—of *providence,* from God; *fatal,* from the soul of the world; of *Nature,* from Heaven; of *prudence,* from man. There are also four judiciary powers in all things being, viz., the intellect, discipline, opinion and sense. Also, there are four rivers of Paradise. Four Gospels, received from four Evangelists, throughout the whole Church. The Hebrews received the chiefest name of God (Spirit), written with four letters. Also the Egyptians, Arabians, Persians, Magicians, Mohametans, Grecians, Tuscans, and Latins, write the name of God with four letters, viz., thus—Thet, Alla, Sire, Orsi, Abdi, θεὸς, Esar, Deus. Hence the Lacedemonians were wont to paint Jupiter with four wings. Hence, also, in Orpheus' Divinity, it is said that Neptune's chariots are drawn with four horses. There are also four kinds of divine furies proceeding from several deities, viz., from the Muses, Dionysius, Apollo, and Venus. Also, the Prophet Ezekiel saw four beasts by the river Chobar, and four cherubims in four wheels. Also, in Daniel, four great beasts did ascend from the sea; and four winds did fight. And in the Revelations, four beasts were full of eyes, before and behind, standing round about the throne of God; and four angels, to whom was given the power to hurt the earth and the sea, did stand upon the four corners of the earth, holding the four winds, that they should not blow upon the earth, nor upon the sea, nor upon any tree.

NUMBER FIVE AND SCALE.

The number Five is of no small force; for it consists of the first even and the first odd: as of a female and male: for an odd number is the male, and the even the female; whence arithmeticians call that the father, and this the mother. Therefore the number five is of no small perfection or virtue, which proceeds from the mixtion of these numbers; it is, also, the just middle of the universal number, viz., ten: for if you divide the number ten, there will be nine and one, or eight and two, and seven and three, or six and four, and every collection makes the number ten. and the exact middle is always the number five. and its equa-distant;

and therefore it is called, by the Hindu Adepts, the number of wedlock, as also of justice, because it divides the number ten in an even scale. There are five senses in man—sight, hearing, smelling, tasting, and feeling; five powers in the soul—vegetative, sensitive, concupiscible, irascible, and rational; five fingers on the hand; five wandering planets in the heavens, according to which there are fivefold terms in every sign. In elements there are five kinds of mixed bodies, viz., stones, metals, plants plant-animals, animals; and so many kinds of animals—as men, four-footed beasts, creeping, swimming, and flying. And there are five kinds by which all things are made of God, viz., essence, the same, another,

THE SCALE OF THE NUMBER FIVE.

The Names of God with five letters. The Name of Christ with five letters,		אליון אלהים יהשוה	Eloim, Elohi, Jhesu,			In the exemplary world.
Five intelligible substances,	Spirits of the first hierarchy, called Gods, or the sons of God,	Spirits of the second hierarchy, called Intelligences,	Spirits of the the third hierarchy, called Angels which are sent,	Souls of celestial bodies,	Heroes and blessed souls.	In the intellectual world.
Five wandering stars, lords of the terms,	turn,	Jupiter,	Mars,	Venus,	Mercury.	In the celestial world.
Five kinds of corruptible things,	Water,	Air,	Fire,	Earth,	A mixed body.	In the elementary world.
Five kinds of mixed bodies,	nimal,	Plant,	Metal,	Stone,	Plant-animal.	
Five senses,	Taste,	Hearing,	Seeing,	Touching,	Smelling.	In the lesser world.
Five corporeal torments,	Deadly bitterness,	Horrible howling,	Terrible darkness,	Unquenchable heat,	A piercing stink.	In the infernal world.

sense, and motion. The swallow brings forth but five young, which she feeds with equity, beginning with the eldest, and so the rest according to their age. For in this number the father Noah found favor with God, and was preserved in the flood of waters. In the virtue of this number, Abraham, being an hundred years old, begat a son of Sarah (Sarah being ninety years old, and a barren woman, and past childbearing), and grew up to be a great people. Hence in time of grace, the name of Divine Omnipotency is called upon in five letters; in time of nature, the name of God was called upon with three letters שדי

Sadai; in time of the law, the ineffable name of God was expressed with four letters יהוה instead of which the Hebrews express, אדני Adonai; in time of grace, the ineffable name of God was written with five letters יהשוה Jeshu which is called upon with no less mystery than that of three letters יֶשֶׁך.

NUMBER SIX AND SCALE.

Six is a number of perfection, because it is the most perfect in nature, in the whole course of numbers, from one to ten; and it alone is so perfect that in the collection of its parts, it results the same, neither wanting nor abounding; for if the parts thereof, viz., the middle, third, and sixth part, which are three, two, one, be gathered tobether, they

THE SCALE OF THE NUMBER SIX.

In the Exemplary World,	אל גבוראלוהים						Names of six letters.
In the Intelligible World,	Seraphim,	Cherubim,	Thrones,	Domina-tions,	Powers,	Virtues;	Six orders of Angels, which are not sent to inferiors.
In the Celestial World,	Saturn,	Jupiter,	Mars,	Venus,	Mercury,	The Moon;	Six planets wandering through the latitude of the Zodiac from the Ecliptic.
In the Elemental World,	Rest,	Thinness,	Sharpness,	Dulness,	Thickness,	Motion;	Six substantial qualities of the elements.
In the Lesser World,	The Intellect,	Memory,	Sense,	Motion,	Life,	Essence;	Six degrees of the mind.
In the Infernal World,	Acteus,	Megalesius	Ormenus,	Lycus,	Nicon,	Mimon;	Six Devils, the authors of all calamities.

perfectly fill up the whole body of six, which perfection all the other numbers want. Hence, by the Hindu Adepts, it is said to be altogether to be applied to generation and marriage, and is called the scale of the world; for the world is made of the number six—neither doth it abound, nor is defective; hence that is, because the world was finished by God the sixth day; for the sixth day God saw all things which he had made, and they were* *very good;* therefore the heaven, and the earth, and all the host thereof, were finished. It is also called the number of man, because

---

* The sixth day, the Eternal Wisdom pronounced all things created by his divine hand to be *"very good."*

the sixth day† man was created.   And it is also the number of our redemption; for on the sixth day Christ suffered for our redemption; whence there is a great affinity between the number six and the cross, labor, and servitude.   Hence it is commanded in the law, that in six days the manna is to be gathered, and work to be done.   Six years the ground was to be sown; and that the Hebrew servant was to serve his master six years.   Six days the glory of the Lord appeared upon Mount Sinai, covering it with a cloud.   The Cherubims had six wings.   Six circles in the firmament: Artic, Antartic, two Tropics, Equinoctial and Ecliptical.   Six wandering planets: Saturn, Jupiter, Mars, Venus, Mercury, the Moon, running through the latitude of the Zodiac on both sides the Ecliptic.   There are six substantial qualities in the elements, viz., sharpness, thinness, motion: and the contrary to these—dullness, thickness, and rest.   There are six differences of position: upwards, downwards, before, behind, on the right side, and on the left side. There are six natural offices, without which nothing can be, viz., magnitude, color, figure, interval, standing, motion.   Also, a solid figure of any four-square thing hath six superfices.   There are six tones of all harmony, viz., five tones, and two half tones which make one tone, which is the sixth.

NUMBER SEVEN AND SCALE.

The number Seven is of various and manifold power; for it consists of one and six, or of two and five, or of three and four; and it hath a unity, as it were the coupling together of two threes: whence if we consider the several parts thereof, and the joining together of them, without doubt we shall confess that it is, as well by the joining together of the parts thereof as by its fullness apart, most full of all majesty. And the Hindu Adepts call it the vehiculum of man's life, which it doth not receive from its parts so, as it perfects by its proper right of its whole—for it contains body and soul; for the body consists of four elements, and is endowed with four qualities: also, the number three respects the soul, by reason of its threefold power, viz., rational, irascible, and concupiscible.   The number seven, therefore, because it consists of three and four joins the soul to the body; and the virtue of this number relates to the generation of men, and it causes man to be received, formed, brought forth, nourished, live, and indeed altogether to subsist; for when the genital seed is received in the womb of the woman, if it remains there seven hours after the effusion of it, it is certain that it will abide there for good; then the first seven days it is coagulated, and is fit to receive the shape of a man; then it produces mature infants,

---

† Hence arose the mystery of a number of the beast, six hundred three score and six, being the number of a man—DCLXVI.

which are called infants of the seventh month, *i. e.,* because they are born the seventh month; after the birth, the seventh hour tries whether it will live or no—for that which will bear the breath of the air after that hour, is conceived will live; after seven days, it casts off the relics of the navel; after twice seven days, its sight begins to move after the light; in the third seventh, it turns its eyes and whole face freely; after seven months, it breeds teeth; after the second seventh month, it sits without fear of falling; after the third seventh month, it begins to speak; after the fourth seventh month, it stands strongly and walks; after the fifth seventh month, it begins to refrain sucking its nurse; after seven years, its first teeth fall, and new are bred, fitter for harder meat, and its speech is perfected; after the second seventh year, boys wax ripe, and then it is a beginning of generation at the third seventh year, they grow to men in stature, and begin to be hairy, and become able and strong for generation; at the fourth seventh year, they cease to grow taller; in the fifth seventh year, they attain to the perfection of their strength; the sixth seventh year, they keep their strength; the seventh seventh year, they attain to their utmost discretion and wisdom, and the perfect age of men; but when they come to the tenth seventh year, where the number seven is taken for a complete number, then they come to the common term of life—the Prophet saying, our age is seventy years. The utmost heights of a man's body is seven feet. There are, also seven degrees in the body, which complete the dimension of its altitude from the bottom to the top, viz., marrow, bone, nerve, vein, artery, flesh and skin. There are seven, which, by the Hindus, are called black members: the tongue, heart, lungs, liver, spleen, and the two kidnies. There are, also, seven principal parts, of the body: the head, breast, hands, feet and the privy members. It is manifest, concerning breath and meat, that, without drawing of the breath, the life doth not remain above seven hours; and they that are starved with famine, live not above seven days.* The veins, also, and arteries, as physicians say, are moved by the seventh number. Also, judgments in diseases are made with greater manifestation upon the seventh day, which physicians call critical, *i. e.,* judicial. The soul, also, receives the body by seven degrees. All difference of voices proceeds to the seventh degree, after which there is the same revolution. Again, there are seven modulations of the voices: ditonus, semiditonus, diatesseron, diapente with a tone, diapente with a half tone, and diapason. There are also, in celestials, a most potent power of the number of seven; for seeing there are four corners of the

---

* There have been some exceptions to this affirmation, one of which fell under my notice of late years: Pyxjmaxybu, Philosopher, Cabalist, and Hindu Physician, lived upwards of two years upon a gooseberry a day in summer, and an oat cake and three glasses of white wine the rest of the season, per day; this gentleman was particularly abstemious in his diet.

Heaven diametrically looking one towards the other, which indeed is accounted a most full and powerful aspect, and consists of the number seven; for it is made with the seventh sign, and makes a cross, the most powerful figure of all, of which we shall speak in its due place— but this you must not be ignorant of, that the number seven hath a great communion with the cross. By the same radiation and number the solstice is distant from winter, and the winter equinoctium from the summer, all which are done by seven signs. There are also seven circles in the Heavens, according to the longitudes of the axle-tree. There are seven stars about the Arctic Pole, greater and lesser, called

THE SCALE OF THE NUMBER SEVEN.

In the Original World,	Ararita,	אדאדירהא		
In the Intelligible World,	צפקאיל Zaphiel,	צדקיאל Zadkiel,	כמאל Camael,	דפאל Raphael,
In the Celestial World.	שבתאי Saturn.	צרק Jupiter,	מאדים Mars,	שמש The Sun.
In the Elementary World,	The lapwing, The cuttle fish, The mole, Lead, The onyx,	The eagle, The dolphin, The hart, Tin The Saphire,	The vulture, The pike, The wolf, Iron, The diamond,	The swan, The sea calf The lion, Gold, The carbuncle,
In the Lesser World,	The right foot, The right ear,	The head, The left ear,	The right hand, The right nostril,	The heart, The right eye,
In the Infernal World,	Hell, ניהבם	The gates of death, רצלטות	The shadow of death, ידעשחוט	The pit of destruction. באדשחת

Binjo; also seven stars called the *Kjuma;* the seven planets, according to those seven days, constituting a week. The Moon is the seventh of the planets, and next to us, observing this number more than the rest, this number dispensing the motion and light thereof; for in twenty-eight days, it runs round the compass of the whole *Zodiac;* which number of days, the number seven with its seven terms, viz. from one to seven, doth make and fill up as much as the several numbers, by adding to the antecedents, and makes four times seven days, in which the Moon runs through and about all the longitude and latitude of the *Zodiac,* by measuring and measuring again: with the like seven days it dispenses its light, by changing it; for the first seven days, unto the middle as it were of the divided world, it increases; the second seven days it fills its whole orb with light; the third, by decreasing, is again contracted into a divided orb; but, after the fourth seven days, it is renewed with the last diminution of its light; and by the same seven days, its disposes the increase and decrease of the sea: for in the first seven of the increase of the moon, it is by little and little lessoned; in the second, by degrees increased; but the third is like the first, and the fourth does the same as the second. It is also applied to Saturn, which ascending from the lower, is the seventh planet, which betokens rest; to which the seventh day is ascribed, which signifies the seven thousandth, wherein, as St. John says, the dragon (which is the Devil) and satan being bound,

THE SCALE OF THE NUMBER SEVEN.

Asser Eheie,	אשד אהיה		The name of God with seven letters.
האביאל Haniel,	מיבאל Michael,	נכדיאל Gabriel;	Seven angels which stand in the presence of God.
כונה Venus,	כוכב Mercury,	לבכה The Moon:	Seven planets.
The dove, Thimallus, The goat, Copper, The emerald,	The Stork, The mullet, The ape, Quicksilver, The achates,	The owl; The sea cat; Cat; Silver; Chrystal;	Seven birds of the planets. Seven fish of the planets. Seven animals of the planets. Seven metals of the planets. Seven stones of the planets.
The privy members, The left nostril.	The left hand. The mouth,	The left foot; The left eye;	Seven integral members distributed to the planets. Seven holes of the head distributed to the planets.
The Clay of death, מיטהין	Perdition, אבח	The depth of the earth. שאול	Seven habitations of infernals, which Rabbi Joseph of Castilia, the Cabalist, describes in the garden of nuts.

men shall be quiet and lead a peaceable life. And the leprous person that was to be cleansed, was sprinkled seven times with the blood of a sparrow; and Elisha the Prophet, as it is written in the second book of Kings, saith unto the leprous person—"Go, and wash thyself seven times in Jordan, and thy flesh shall be made whole, and thou shalt be cleansed."—Also, it is a number of repentance and remission. And Christ, with seven petitions, finished his speech of our satisfaction. It is called the number of liberty, because the seventh year, the Hebrew servant did challenge liberty for himself. It is also more suitable to divine praises; whence the Prophet saith—"Seven times a day do I praise thee, because of thy righteous judgments."—It is moreover called the number of revenge, as says the Scripture—"*And Cain shall be revenged sevenfold."* And the *Palmist* says—"Render unto our neighbors sevenfold into their bosom their reproach." Hence there are seven wickednesses, as saith Solomon: and seven wickeder spirits taken, are read of in the Gospel. It signifies, also, the time of the present circle, because it is finished in the space of seven days. Also it is consecrated to the Holy Ghost, which the Prophet Isaiah describes to be sevenfold, according to his gift, viz. the spirit of wisdom and understanding, the spirit of counsel and strength, the spirit of knowledge and holiness, the spirit of fear of the Lord, which we read in Zachariah to be the *seven eyes of God*. There are also seven angels, spirits standing in the presence of God, as is read in Tobias, and in then Revelation: seven lamps did burn before the throne of God, and seven golden candlesticks, and in the middle thereof was one like unto the Son of Man, and he had in his right hand seven stars. Also, there were seven spirits before the throne of God, and seven angels stood before the throne, and there were given to them seven trumpets. And he saw a lamb having seven horns and seven eyes; and he saw the book sealed with seven seals; and when the seventh seal was opened, there was made silence in Heaven.

Now, by all that has been said, it is apparent that the number seven, amongst the other numbers, may be deservedly said to be most full of efficacy. Moreover, the number seven hath great conformity with the number twelve; for as three and four make seven, so thrice four makes twelve, which are the numbers of the celestial planets and signs resulting from the same root; and by the number three partaking of the Divinity, and by the number four of the nature of inferior things. There is in sacred writ a very great observance of this number before all others, and many, and very great are the mysteries thereof; many we have decreed to reckon up here, repeating them out of holy writ, by which it will easily appear that the number seven doth signify a certain fulness of sacred mysteries; for we read, in Genesis, that the seventh day was the day of rest of the Lord; that Enoch, a pious holy man, was the seventh from Adam; and that there was another seventh man from Adam, a wicked man, by name Lamech, that had two wives; and that the sin of Cain should be abolished the seventh generation, as it is written—Cain shall be punished sevenfold; and that he who shall slay Cain, shall be revenged sevenfold; to which the master of the history collects that there were seven sins of Cain. Also, of all clean beasts seven, and seven were brought to the ark, as also of fowls; and after seven days the Lord rained upon the earth; and upon the seventh day the fountains of the deep were broken up, and the waters covered the earth. Also, Abraham gave to Abimelech seven ewe lambs; and Jacob served seven years for Leah, and seven more for Rachel; and seven days the people of Israel bewailed the death of Jacob. Moreover, we read, in the same place, of seven kine; and seven years of corn;

seven years of plenty, and seven years of scarcity. And in Exodus, the Sabbath of Sabbaths, the holy rest to the Lord, is commanded to be on the seventh day; also, on the seventh day Moses ceased to pray. On the seventh day there shall be a solemnity of the Lord; the seventh year the servant shall go out free; seven days let the calf and the lamb be with its dam; the seventh year, let the ground that hath been sown six years be at rest; the seventh day shall be a holy Sabbath, and a rest; the seventh day, because it is the Sabbath, shall be called holy. In Leviticus, the seventh day also shall be more observed, and be more holy; and the first day of the seventh month shall be a Sabbath of memorial; seven days shall the sacrifices be offered to the Lord; seven days shall the holy days of the Lord be celebrated; seven days in a year everlastingly in the generations. In the seventh month you shall celebrate feasts, and shall dwell in tabernacles seven days; seven times he shall sprinkle himself before the Lord that hath dipped his finger in blood; he that is cleansed from the leprosy, shall dip seven times in the blood of a sparrow; seven days shall she be washed with running water that is menstruous; seven times he shall dip his finger in the blood of a bullock; seven times I will smite you for your sins. In Deuteronomy, seven people possessed the Land of Promise. There is also read, a seventh year of remission; and seven candles set up on the south side of the candlesticks. And in Numbers it is read, that the sons of Israel offered up seven ewe lambs without spot; and that seven days they did eat unleavened bread; and that sin was expiated with seven lambs and a goat; and that the seventh day was celebrated, and holy, and the first day of the seventh month was observed and kept holy; and the seventh month of the Feast of Tabernacles; and seven calves were offered on the seventh day; and Balaam erected seven altars; seven days Mary, the sister of Aaron, went forth leprous out of the camp; seven days he that touched a dead carcass was unclean. And in Joshua, seven priests carried the ark of the covenant before the host; and seven days they went round the cities; and seven trumpets were carried by seven priests; and on the seventh day, the seven priests sounded the trumpets. And in the book of Judges, Abessa reigned in Israel seven years; Sampson kept his nuptials seven days, and the seventh day he put forth a riddle to his wife; he was bound with seven green withes; seven locks of his head were shaved off; seven years were the children of Israel oppressed by the King of Maden. And in the books of the Kings, Elias prayed seven times, and at the seventh time beheld a little cloud; seven days the children of Israel pitched over against the Syrians, and in the seventh day of the battle were joined; seven years' famine was threatened to David, for the people's murmuring; and seven times the child sneezed that was raised by Elisha; and seven men were crucified together, in the days of the first harvest; Naaman was made clean with seven washings, by Elisha; the seventh month Goliath was slain. And in Hester we read that the King of Persia had seven eunuchs. And in Tobias, seven men were coupled with Sarah, the daughter of Raguel. And in Daniel, Nebuchadnezzar's furnace was heated seven times hotter than it was used to be; and seven lions were in the den, and the seventh day came Nebuchadnezzar. In the book of Job there is mention of the seven sons of Job; and seven days and nights Job's friends sat with him on the earth; and in the same place—"In seven troubles no evil shall come near thee." In Ezra, we read of Artaxerxes's seven counsellors; and in the same place, the trumpet sounded; the seventh month of the Feast of Tabernacles was, in Ezra's time, whilst the children of Israel were in the cities; and on the first day of the seventh month, Esdras read the law to the people. And in the Psalms, David praised the Lord seven times in the day; silver is tried seven times; and he renders to his neighbours sevenfold into their bosoms. And Solomon saith, that Wisdom hath hewn herself seven pillars; seven men that can render a reason; seven abominations which the Lord abhors; seven abominations in the heart of an enemy; seven overseers; seven eyes beholding. Isaiah numbers up seven gifts of the Holy Ghost; and seven women shall take hold on a man. And in Jeremiah, if she that hath borne seven, languishes, she has given up the ghost. In Ezekiel, the Prophet continued sad for seven days. In Zachariah, seven lamps, and seven pipes to those seven lamps; and seven eyes running to and fro through the whole earth; and seven eyes on one stone; and the fast of the seventh day is turned into joy. And in Micah, seven shepherds are raised against the Assyrians. Also, in the Gospel, we read of seven blessings; and seven virtues, to which seven vices are opposed; seven petitions of the Lord's Prayers; seven words of Christ upon the cross; seven words of the blessed Virgin Mary; seven loaves distributed by the Lord; seven baskets of fragments; seven brothers having one wife; seven disciples of the Lord who were fishers; seven water pots in Cana of Galilee; seven woes which the Lord threatens to hypocrites; seven devils cast out of the unclean woman, and seven wickeder devils taken in after that which was cast out; also, seven years Christ was fled into Egypt; and the seventh hour the fever left the governor's son. And in the canonical epistles, James describes seven degrees of wisdom; and Peter, seven degrees of virtues. And in the Acts, we reckon seven deacons, and seven disciples, chosen by the Apostles. Also in the Revelations, there are many mysteries relating to this number; for there we read of seven candlesticks, seven stars, seven crowns, seven churches, seven spirits before the throne, seven rivers of Egypt, seven seals, seven marks, seven horns, seven eyes, seven spirits of God, seven angels with seven trumpets, seven horns of the dragon, seven heads of the dragon, which had seven diadems, also seven plagues, and seven vials which were given to every one of the seven angels, seven heads of the scarlet beast, seven mountains and seven kings sitting upon them, and seven thunders uttered their voices.

Moreover, this number hath much power; as in natural so in sacred ceremonial, and also in other things; therefore the seven days are related hither; also the seven planets, the seven stars called Pleiades, the seven ages of the world, the seven changes of man, the seven liberal arts, and as many mechanic, and so many forbidden; seven colours, seven metals, seven holes in the head of a man, seven pairs of nerves, seven mountains in the city of Rome, seven Roman kings, seven civil wars, seven wise men in the time of Jeremiah, seven wise men of Greece; also Rome did burn seven days by Nero; by seven kings were slain ten thousand martyrs; there were seven sleepers; and seven principal churches of Rome.

NUMBER EIGHT AND SCALE.

The Adepts of Indian call Eight the number of justice, and fulness: first, because it is first of all divided into numbers equally even, viz.

THE SCALE OF THE NUMBER EIGHT

The name of God with eight letters.	Eloa Vadaath אלוה ודעת				Jehova Vedaath יהוה ודעת				In the original world.
Eight rewards of the blessed.	Inheritance,	Incorruption,	Power,	Victory,	The vision of God,	Grace,	A kingdom,	Joy;	In the intelligible world.
Eight visible heavens,	The starry heaven,	The heaven of Saturn,	The heaven of Jupiter,	The heaven of Mars,	The heaven of the Sun,	The heaven of Venus,	The heaven of Mercury,	The heaven of the Moon;	In the celestial world.
Eight particular qualities,	The dryness of the earth,	The coldness of water,	The moisture of air,	The heat of fire,	The heat of air,	The moisture of water,	The dryness of fire,	The coldness of earth;	In the elementary world
Eight kinds of blessed men,	The peace makers,	They that hunger and thirst after righteousness	The meek,	They which are persecuted for righteousness sake,	Pure in heart,	Merciful	Poor in spirit,	Mourners;	In the lesser world.
Eight punishments of the damned.	Prison,	Death,	Judgment,	The wrath of God,	Darkness,	Indignation.	Tribulation.	Anguish;	In the infernal world.

into four; and that division is, by the same reason, made into twice two, viz. twice two twice; and by reason of this equality of division it took to itself the name of justice. But the other received the name of fulness, by reason of the contexture of the corporeal solidity, since the first makes a solid body. Hence that custom of Orpheus swearing by the eight deities, if at any time he would beseech Divine justice, whose names are these:—Fire, Water, Earth, the Heaven, Moon, Sun, Phanes, and Night. There are only eight visible spheres of the heavens. Also, by it the property of corporeal nature is signified, which Orpheus comprehends in eight of his sea songs: this is also called the covenant of circumcision, which was commanded to be done by the Jews the eighth day.

There were also, in the old law, eight ornaments of the priest, viz. a breastplate, a coat, a girdle, a mitre, a robe, an ephod, a girdle of the ephod, and a golden plate. Hither belong the number to eternity, and the end of the world, because it follows the number seven, which is the mystery of time. Hence, also, the number of blessedness, as you may see in Matthew. It is also called the number of safety, and conservatism; for there were so many souls of the sons of Jesse, from which David was the eighth.

NUMBER NINE AND SCALE.

There are nine orders of blessed angels, viz. Seraphim, Cherubim, Thrones, Dominations, Powers, Virtues, Principalities, Archangels, and

THE SCALE OF THE NUMBER NINE.

The name of God with nine letters,	Jehovah Sabbaoth, יהוה צבאוה			Jehovah Zidkenu, יהוהצרקבו			Elohim Gibor, אלוהים גיפוד			In the Original world.
Nine quires of angels, Nine angels ruling the heavens,	Sera-phim, Merat-tron,	Che-rubim Opha-niel,	Thrones Zaph-kiel,	Domin-ations, Zad-kiel,	Powers Camael	Virtues Ra-phael,	Princi-palities Haniel,	Arch-angels, Michael	Angels Gabriel	In the intelligible world.
Nine moveable spheres,	The primum mobile,	The starry heaven	The sphere of Saturn,	The sphere of Jupiter	The sphere of Mars,	The sphere of the Sun,	The sphere of Venus,	The sphere of Mercury,	The sphere of the Moon;	In the celestial world.
Nine stones representing the nine quires of angels,	Saph-ire,	Eme-rald.	Car-buncle,	Beryl,	Onyx,	Chryso-lite.	Jasper	Topaz,	Sardis;	In the elementary world.
Nine senses inward and outward together,	Mem-ory,	Cogita-tive,	Imagin-ative,	Com-mon sense,	Hear-ing,	Seeing.	Smell-ing,	Tasting	Touch-ing;	In the lesser world.
Nine orders of devils,	False Spirits,	Spirits of lying,	Vessels of iniquity	Aven-gers of wick-edness,	Jug-glers,	Airy Powers	Furies sowing mis-chief,	Sifters or triers,	Tempt-ers, or ens-narers;	In the infernal world.

Angels, which Ezekiel figures out by nine stones, which are the sapphire, emerald, carbuncle, beryl, onyx, chrysolite, jasper, topaz, and sardis. This number hath also a great and occult mystery of the cross; for the ninth hour our Lord Jesus Christ breathed out his spirit. The astrologers also take notice of the number nine in the ages of men, no otherwise than they do of seven, which they call climacterical years, which are eminent for some remarkable change. Yet sometimes it signifies imperfectness and incompleteness, because it does not attain to the perfection of the number ten, but is less by one, without which it is deficient, as Austin interprets it of the ten lepers. Neither is the longitude of nine cubits of Og, King of Basan, who is a type of the devil without a mystery.

NUMBER TEN AND SCALE.

The number Ten is called every number, or an universal number, complete, signifying the full course of life; for beyond that we cannot

SCALE OF NUMBER TEN.

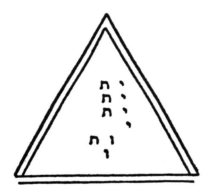

number but by replication; and it either implies all numbers within itself, or explains them by itself, and its own, by multiplying them; wherefore it is accounted to be of manifold religion and power, and is applied to the purging of souls. Hence the antients called ceremonies Denary, because they were to be expiated and to offer sacrifices, and were to abstain from some certain things for ten days.

There are ten sanguine parts of man: the menstrues, the sperm, the plasonatic spirit, the mass, the humours, the organical body, the vegetative part, the sensitive part, reason, and the mind. There are, also, ten simple integral parts constituting man: the bone, cartilage, nerve, fibre, ligament, artery, vein, membrane, flesh, and skin. There are, also, ten parts of which a man consists intrinsically: the spirit, the brain, the lungs, the heart, the liver, the gall, the spleen, the kidnies, the testicles, and the matrix. There are ten curtains in the temple, ten strings in the psaltery, ten musical instruments with which the psalms were sung, the names wherof were—*neza*, on which their odes were sung; *nablum*, the same as organs; *mizmor*, on which the Psalms; *sir*, on which the Canticles; *tehila*, on which orations; *beracha*, on which benedictions; *halel*, on which praises; *hodaia*, on which thanks; *asre*, on which the felicity of any one; *hallelujah*, on which the praises of God only, and contemplations. There were also ten singers of psalms, viz. *Adam, Abraham, Melchisedeck, Moses, Asaph, David, Solomon,* and *the three sons of Chora.* There are, also, ten commandments. And then tenth day after the ascension of Christ, the Holy Ghost came down. Lastly, this is the number, in which Jacob, wrestling with the Angel all night, overcame, and, at the rising of the sun, was blessed, and called by the

THE SCALE OF NUMBER TEN.

In the original,	יחוהיהויהי The name of Jehovah of ten letters collected.			ואו הא The name of Jehovah of ten letters,	
	אהיח Eheie,	ויהוה Jod Jehovah,	יהוהאלהים Jehovah Elohim	אל El.	אלהימניבר Elohim Gibor,
	כתר Ketber,	חכמה Hochmah,	בינה Binah,	הכד Hesed,	נבורה Geburah,
In the intelligible world,	Seraphim,	Cherubim,	Thrones,	Dominations,	Powers,
	Hajothhaka- dos.	Orphanim,	Aralim.	Hasmallim,	Seraphim,
	Merattron,	Jophiel,	Zaphkiel,	Zadkiel,	Camael,
In the celestial world,	Reschith haga- llalim, the pri- mum mobile,	Masloth, the sphere of the Zodiac,	Sabbathi, the sphere of Saturn	Zedeck, the sphere of Jupiter,	Madim, the sphere of Mars,
In the elementary world,	A dove,	A lizard,	A dragon,	An eagle,	A horse,
In the lesser world,	Spirit,	Brain,	Spleen,	Liver,	Gall,
In the infernal world,	False gods,	Lying spirits,	Vessels of iniquity.	Revengers of wickedness,	Jugglers,

name of Israel. In this number, Joshua overcame thirty-one kings; and David overcame Goliath and the Philistines; and Daniel escaped the danger of the lions. This number is also circular, as unity; because, being heaped together, returns into a unity, from whence it had its beginning; and it is the end and perfection of all numbers, and the beginning of tens. As the number ten flows back into a unity, from whence it proceeded, so every thing that is flowing is returned back to that from which it had the beginning of its flux; so water returns to the sea, from whence it had its beginning; the body returns to the earth, from whence it was taken; time returns into eternity, from whence it flowed; the spirit shall return to God, who gave it; and, lastly, every creature returns to nothing, from whence it was created.* Neither is it supported but by the word of God, in whom all things are hid, and all things with the number ten, and by the number ten, make a round, as Adepts say, taking their beginning from God, and ending in him. God, therefore (that first unity, or one thing), before he communicated himself to inferiors, diffused himself first into the first of numbers, viz. the number three; then into the number ten, as into ten ideas and measures of making all numbers and all things, which the Hebrews call ten attributes, and account ten divine names; from which cause

THE SCALE OF NUMBER TEN.

יוד הא Extended,		אלהימצבאות The name Elohim Sabaoth;			The name of God with ten letters.
אליה Eloha,	יחוהצבאות JehovahSaboath	אלהימצבאות Elohim Saboath,	שדי Sadai,	אדני Adonaimelech	Ten names of God.
תפארת Tiphereth,	נצח Nezah,	הוד Hod,	יסוד Jeson,	מלכות Malchuth;	Ten Sephiroth.
Virtues,	Principalities,	Archangels,	Angels,	Blessed souls;	Ten orders of the blessed, according to Dionysius.
Malachim,	Elohim,	Ben Elohim,	Cherubim,	Issim;	Ten orders of the blessed, according to the traditions of men.
Raphael,	Haniel,	Michael,	Gabriel,	The soul of Messiah;	Ten angels ruling.
Schemes, the sphere of the Sun,	Noga, the sphere of Venus,	Cochab, the sphere of Mercury,	Levanah, the sphere of the Moon,	Holom Jesodoth, the sphere of the elements;	Ten Spheres of the world.
Lion,	Man,	The fox,	Bull,	Lamb;	Ten animals consecrated to the gods.
Heart,	Kidnies,	Lungs,	Genitals,	Matrix;	Ten parts intrinsical of man.
Airy Powers,	Furies, the seminaries of evil,	Sifters, or triers,	Tempters, or ensnarers,	Wicked souls bearing rule;	Ten orders of the damned.

there cannot be a further number. Hence all tens have some divine thing in them, and in the law are required as his own, together with the first fruits, as the original of all things and beginning of numbers, and every tenth is as the end given to him, who is the beginning and end of all things.

*At the last, the elements gave up what they have ever received; the sea gives up her dead, the fire gives up its fuel; the earth gives up the seminal virtue, etc.; and the air gives up whatever voice, sound or impression it has received, so that not an oath, lie, or secret blasphemy, but what will appear as clear as noonday light at the great day of God.

NUMBER ELEVEN AND TWELVE.

The number Eleven, as it exceeds number ten, which is the number of the commandments, so it falls short of the number Twelve, which is of grace and perfection; therefore it is called the number of sins, and the penitent. Now the number twelve is divine, and that whereby the celestials are measured.* It is, also, the number of signs in the Zodiac,

---

* The use of these Scales, in the composition of Talismans, Seals, Rings, etc., must be obvious to every student upon inspection, and are indispensably necessary to the producing of any effect whatever that the Adept may propose to himself; for, as I have before observed, all things were formed according to the proportion of numbers, this seeming to be the principal pattern in the mind of the Creator; therefore, when at any time ye go about any work or experiment in Celestial Magic, you are to have especial regard to the rule of numbers and proportions. For example, if you would obtain the celestial influence of any star, you are, first of all, to observe at what time that star is powerful in the heavens, I mean in good aspect with the benefices, and ruling in the day and hour appropriated to the planet, and in fortunate places of the figure; then we are to observe what divine names are ruling the intelligences, or spirits, to which the said planets are subject with their characters (which you may see at large in the Magical Tables of Numbers); then, by referring to the above Tables of the Scales, we may see, by inspection, to what numbers are attributed divine names, and, under them, the orders of the intelligences—the heavenly spheres—elements and their properties—animals, metals, and stones—powers of the soul—senses of man—virtues—the princes of the evil spirits—places of punishments—degrees of the damned souls—degrees of torments hereafter—and everything that is either in heaven, or earth, or hell;—all our senses, motions, qualities, virtues, words, or works, are submitted to the proportions of numbers, as you may see fully exemplified in the different Scales of the Numbers; and all things that are knowable are demonstrable by them, and are attributed to them: therefore great is the knowledge and wisdom to be derived from numbers. Therefore the artist must be well acquainted with their virtues and properties—by them there is a way open for the knowing and understanding of all things; therefore let him diligently contemplate these Scales and likewise what I have set down on pages 69, 70 and 71, preceding the Scales, where I have upon good authority explained sufficiently the extent and force of formal numbers, which ought to be well understood and attentively considered, as the ground and foundation of all thy operations in this science, without which you are defrauded of the desired effect; therefore whenever ye intend to set about any Magical work, whether it be an image, or ring, or tablet, or mirror, or amulet, or any other instrument, you are to note first the site, order, number, and government of the intelligence and his planet, his measure of time, revolution in the heavens, etc.; likewise you are to engrave or write upon it its number, intelligence, or spirit, either for a good or bad effect, with the suitable characters and tables; likewise the effect desired, with the divine names congruent thereto; so that your operations may be strong, powerful, and suitable to the constellation and star, both in time, number, and proportion; with a due and attentive observation of all that I have written concerning this, without which all your operations could never be brought to have the effect desired; and ye are to mind that whenever such an instrument is perfected, that it is the more powerful when the planet or constellation (under which it was constructed) is ruling and potent in the Heavens; for at that time, whatever ye desire to bring to perfection by the said Talisman, as a medium and instrument, shall by no means be *prevented or hindered. Therefore, take this as a general rule, that all magical instruments whatsoever have no power in themselves farther than as they are formed under the influences, and according to the times and numbers of their proper stars and constellations; hence is derived the title I give this Book, viz., the Constellatory Art, or Talismanic Magic. Those who would further consider the power, virtue, extent, and harmony of numbers, let them read Kujinuniza, Gzuno, Bzuninuna, Zunzikin, etc., who all agree in the virtues lying hid in numbers; and without the knowledge of which no man can be a true Adept in Magic.*

THE SCALE OF NUMBER TWELVE.

			הוא Holy.	בריר Blessed,	הקדש He,	
The names of God with twelve letters.						
The great name returned back into twelve banners.	יהוה	יהוש	יוהה	הוהי	השיה	ההיו
Twelve orders of blessed spirits.	Seraphim,	Cherubim,	Thrones,	Dominations,	Powers,	Virtues,
Twelve angels ruling over the twelve signs.	Malchidial,	Asmodel,	Ambriel,	Muriel,	Verchie',	Hamaliel,
Twelve tribes.	Dan,	Ruben,	Judah	Manasseh,	Asher,	Simeon,
Twelve prophets.	Malachi,	Haggai,	'Zachariah,	Amos,	Hosea,	Micha,
Twelve apostles.	Matthias,	Thaddeus,	Simon,	John,	Peter,	Andrew,
Twelve signs of the Zodiac.	Aries,	Taurus,	Gemini,	Cancer,	Leo,	Virgo,
Twelve months.	March,	April,	May,	June,	July,	August,
Twelve plants.	Sang,	Upright vervain,	Bending vervain,	Comfrey,	Ladies' seal,	Calamint,
Twelve stones.	Sardonius,	A cornelian,	Topaz,	Calcedony,	Jasper,	Emerald,
Twelve principal members.	Head,	Neck,	Arms,	Breast,	Heart,	Belly,
Twelve degrees of the damned and of devils.	False gods,	Lying spirits,	Vessels of iniquity,	Revengers of wickedness,	Jugglers,	Airy powers,

THE SCALE OF NUMBER TWELVE.

		אבבגורותתחקרש Father, Son, Holy Ghost,				In the original world.
וחדי	יוהח	יהיה	היהו	חיוה	תחוי	
Principalities,	Archangels,	Angels,	Innocents,	Martyrs,	Confessors.	In the intelligible world.
Zuriel,	Barbiel,	Adnachiel,	Hanael,	Gabriel,	Barchiel.	
Issachar,	Benjamin,	Napthalin.	Gad,	Zabulon,	Ephraim.	
Jonah,	Obadiah,	Zephaniah,	Nahum,	Habakkuk,	Joel.	
Bartholomew,	Philip.	James the elder,	Thomas,	Matthew.	James the younger.	
Libra,	Scorpius,	Sagittarius.	Capricorn,	Aquarius,	Pisces.	In the celestial world.
September,	October,	November	December,	January,	February.	In the elemental world.
Scorpion grass,	Mugwort,	Pimpernel,	Dock,.	Dragonwort,	Aristolochy.	
Beryl,	Amethyst,	Hyacinth,	Chrysophrasus,	Chrystal	Sapphire.	
Kidnies,	Genitals,.	Hams,	Knees,	Leg	Feet.	In the elementary world.
Furies, the sowers of evil,	Sifters, or triers,	Tempters, or ensnarers,	Witches,	Apostates,	Infidels.	In the infernal world.

over which there are twelve angels as chief, supported by the irrigation of the great name of God. In twelve years, also, Jupiter perfects his course; and the Moon daily runs through twelve degrees. There are, also, twelve chief joints in the body of man, viz. in hands, elbows, shoulders, thighs, knees, and vertebræ of the feet. There is, also, a great power of the number twelve in divine mysteries. God chose twelve families of Israel, and set over them twelve princes; so many stones were placed in the midst of Jordan; and God commanded that so many should be set on the breast of the priest. Twelve lions did bear the brazen sea that was made by Solomon; there was so many fountains in Helim; and so many Apostles of Christ set over the twelve tribes; and twelve thousand people were set apart and chosen.

CHARACTERS AND NUMBERS.

The Hebrew characters have marks of numbers attributed to them far more excellent than any other language, since the greatest mysteries lie in the Hebrew letters, as is handled concerning these in that part of Cabala which I called Junymbyn. Now the principal Hebrew letters are in number twenty-two, whereof five have various other certain figures in the end of a word, which, therefore, they call the five ending letters, which being added to them aforesaid, make twenty-seven; which being then divided into three degrees, signify units, which are in the first degree—tens, which are in the second—and hundreds, which are in the third degree. Now every one, if they are marked with a great character, signifies so many thousands, as here—

3000	2000	1000
ג	ב	א

The classes of the Hebrew numbers are these which follow:—

9	8	7	6	5	4	3	2	1
ט	ח	ז	ו	ה	ד	ג	ב	א
90	80	70	60	50	40	30	20	10
צ	פ	ע	ס	נ	מ	ל	כ	י
900	800	700	600	500	400	300	200	100
ץ	ף	ן	ם	ך	ת	ש	ר	ק

Sometimes the final letters are not used, but we write thus:

1000	900	800	700	600	500
א	קתת	תת	תש	תר	קת

And by those simple figures, and by the joining them together, they describe all other compound numbers: as eleven, twelve, an hundred and ten, an hundred and eleven, by adding to the number ten those which are units; and in the like manner to the rest, after their manner; yet we describe the fifteenth number not by ten and five, but six, viz. by nine and　　,נו ; and that out of honor to the Divine name, יה, which signifies fifteen, lest that sacred name should be abused to profane things. Likewise, the Egyptians, AEthiopians, Chaldeans, and Arabians have their marks of numbers which serve for the making of magical characters; but the Chaldeans mark their numbers with the letters of their alphabet, after the manner of the Hindu Adepts.   In this volume of Constellatory Art and Talismanic and Art Magic will be found some very rare characters, which I have figured in the following manner:—

1	2	3	4	5	6	7	8	9

10	20	30	40	50	60	70	80	90

And those marks being downwards, to the right hand, make hundreds; to the left, thousands, viz.

100	200	300	400	500	600	700	800	900

1000	2000	3000	4000	5000	6000	7000	8000	9000

And by the composition and mixture of these characters, other compound numbers are most elegantly made, as you may perceive by these few:—

1510	1511	1471	1486	2421

1801

MAGIC TABLES OF PLANETS.

There are certain magic tables of numbers distributed to the seven planets, which they call the sacred tables of the planets; because, being rightly formed, they are endued with many great virtues of the heavens, insomuch that they represent the divine order of the celestial numbers, impressed upon them by the *ideas* of the divine mind, by means of the soul of the world, and the sweet harmony of those celestial rays; signifying, according to proportion, supercelestial intelligences, which can no other way be expressed than by the marks of numbers, letters, and characters; for *material* numbers and figures can do nothing in the mysteries of hidden things, but representatively by *formal* numbers and figures, as they are governed and informed by intelligences and divine enumerations, which unite the extremes of the matter and spirit to the will of the elevated soul, receiving (through great affection, by the celestial power of the operator) a virtue and power from God, applied through the soul of the universe; and the observation of celestial constellations to a *matter* fit for a form, the mediums being disposed by the skill and industry of the magician.

But now I will hasten to explain each particular table.* The first table is assigned to the planet Saturn, and consists of a square of three, containing the particular numbers of nine, and in every line three every way, and through each diameter making fifteen—the whole sum of numbers forty-five; over this are set such divine names as fill up the numbers with an intelligence, to what is good, and a spirit to bad; and out of the same numbers are drawn the seal and character of Saturn, and of the spirits thereof, such as is beneath ascribed to the table.

Now this table being with a fortunate Saturn, engraven on a plate of lead, helps child-birth; and to make any man safe or powerful; and to cause success of petitions with princes and powers; but if it be done, Saturn being unfortunate, it hinders buildings, planting, and the like, and casts a man from honours and dignities, causes discord, quarreling, and disperses an army.

The second is the table of Jupiter, which consists of a square drawn into itself; it contains sixteen particular numbers, and in every line and diameter four, making thirty-four; the sum of all is one hundred and thirty-six. There are over it divine names, with an intelligence to that which is good, and a spirit to bad; and out of it is drawn the character of Jupiter and the spirits thereof; if this is engraven on a plate of silver, with Jupiter being powerful and ruling in the heavens, it conduces to gain riches and favour, love, peace, and concord, and to appease ene-

---

* For the figure of the Tables, Seals, Characters, etc., of the Seven Planets, see the Plates.

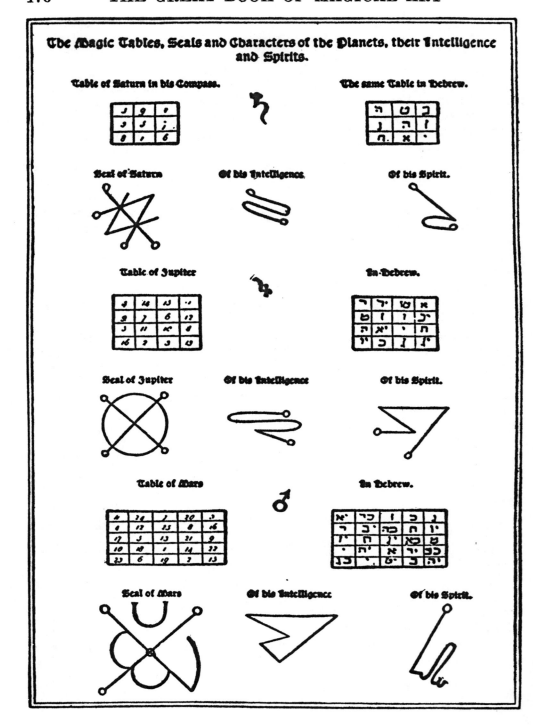

The Magic Tables, Seals and Characters of the Planets, their Intelligence and Spirits.

Table of the Sun in his Compass.

The same in Hebrew.

Character of the Seal of the Sun

Of his Intelligence

Of his Spirit.

Table of Venus in her Compass

In Hebrew.

Seal of Venus

Her Intelligence

Her Spirit

Her Intelligences.

mies, and to confirm honours, dignities, and counsels; and dissolves enchantments if engraven on a coral.

The third table belongs to Mars, which is made of a square of five, containing twenty-five numbers, and of these, in every side and diameter, five, which makes sixty-five, and the sum of all is three hundred and twenty-five; and there are over it divine names with an intelligence to good, and a spirit to evil, and out of it is drawn the characters of Mars and of his spirits. These, with *Mars* fortunate, being engraven on an iron plate, or sword, makes a man potent in war and judgment, and petitions, and terrible to his enemies; and victorious over them; and if engraven upon the stone correola, it stops blood, and the menstrues; but if it be engraven, with *Mars* being unfortunate, on a plate of red brass, it prevents and hinders buildings—it casts down the powerful from dignities, honours, and riches—causes discord and hatred amongst men and beasts—drives away bees, pigeons, and fish—and hinders mills from working, *i. e.,* binds them;—it likewise renders hunters and fighters unfortunate—causes barrenness in men and women—and strikes a terror into our enemies, and compels them to submit.

The fourth table is of the *Sun,* and is made of a square of six, and contains thirty-six particular numbers, whereof six in every side and diameter produce one hundred and eleven, and the sum of all is six hundred and sixty-six; there are over it divine names, with an intelligence to what is good, and a spirit to what is evil, and out of it is drawn the character of the Sun and of his spirits. This being engraven on a plate of pure gold, Sol being fortunate, renders him that wears it renowned, amiable, acceptable, potent in all his works, and equals him to a king, elevating his fortunes, and enabling him to do whatever he will. But with an unfortunate Sun, it makes one a tyrant, proud, ambitious, insatiable, and finally to come to an ill ending.

The fifth table is of Venus; consisting of a square of seven, drawn into itself, viz. of forty-nine numbers, whereof seven on each side and diameter make one hundred and seventy-five, and the sum of all is one thousand two hundred and twenty-five; there are, likewise, over it divine names, with an intelligence to good, and a spirit to evil; and there is drawn out of it the character Venus, and her spirits. This being engraven on a plate of silver, Venus being fortunate, promotes concord, ends strife, procures the love of women, helps conception, is good against barrenness, gives ability for generation, dissolves enchantments, causes peace between man and woman, and makes all kinds of animals fruitful, and likewise cattle; and being put into a dove or pigeon house, causes an increase; it likewise drives away melancholy distempers, and causes joyfulness; and this being carried about travellers, makes them fortunate. But if it be found upon brass, Venus being unfortunate, it acts contrary to all that has been said.

The sixth table is of Mercury, resulting from a square of eight drawn into itself, containing sixty-four numbers, whereof eight on every side and by both diameters make two hundred and sixty, and the sum of all is two thousand and eighty; and over it are set divine names, with an intelligence to good, with a spirit to bad, and from it is drawn a character of Mercury, and the spirits thereof; and if, with Mercury being fortunate, you engrave it upon silver, tin, or yellow brass, or write it upon virgin parchment, it renders the bearer thereof grateful, acceptable, and fortunate to do what he pleases: it brings gain, and prevents poverty; helps the memory, understanding, and divination, and to the understanding of occult things by dreams; but with an unfortunate Mercury does everything contrary to this.

The seventh and last table is of the Moon: it consists of a square of nine, having eighty-one numbers in every side, and diameter nine, producing three hundred and sixty-nine; and the sum of all is three thousand three hundred and twenty-one. There are over it divine names, with an intelligence to what is good, and a spirit to evil; and from it are drawn the characters of the Moon and the spirits thereof. This, the Moon being fortunate, engraven on silver, makes the bearer amiable, pleasant, cheerful, and honoured, removing all malice and ill-will; it causes security in the journey, increases of riches, and health of body, drives away enemies and other evil things from what place soever thou shalt wish them to be expelled. But if the Moon be unfortunate, and it be engraven on a plate of lead, wherever it shall be buried it makes that place unfortunate, and the inhabitants thereabouts, as also ships, rivers, fountains, and mills; and it makes every man unfortunate against whom it shall be directly done, making fly his place of abode (and even his country) where it shall be buried; and it hinders physicians and orators, and all men whatsoever in their office, against whom it shall be made.

Now how the seals and characters of the planets are drawn from these tables, the wise searcher, and he who shall understand the verifying of these tables, shall easily find out.

Here follow the divine names corresponding with the numbers of the planets, with the names of the intelligences and dæmons, or spirits, subject to those names.

It is to be understood that the intelligences are the presiding good angels that are set over the planets; but that the spirits or dæmons, with their names, seals, or characters, are never inscribed upon any Talisman, except to execute any evil effect, and that they are subject to the intelligences, or good spirits; and again, when the spirits and their characters are used, it will be more conducive to the effect to add some divine name appropriate to that effect which we desire.

The Magic Tables, Seals and Characters of the Planets, their Intelligence and Spirits.

Table of Mercury in his Compass.

8	58	59	5	4	62	63	1
49	15	14	52	53	11	10	56
41	23	22	44	45	19	18	48
32	34	35	29	28	38	39	25
40	26	27	37	36	30	31	33
17	47	46	20	21	43	42	24
9	55	54	12	13	51	50	16
64	2	3	61	60	6	7	57

The same in Hebrew.

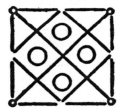

Seal or Character of Mercury.

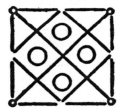

Character of the Intelligence of Mercury.

Character of the Spirit of Mercury.

The Magic Tables, Seals and Characters of the Planets, their Intelligence and Spirits.

Table of the Moon in her Compass.

37	78	29	70	21	62	13	54	5
6	38	79	30	71	22	63	14	46
47	7	39	80	31	72	23	55	15
16	48	8	40	81	32	64	24	56
57	17	49	9	41	73	33	65	25
26	58	18	50	1	42	74	34	66
67	27	59	10	51	2	43	75	35
36	68	19	60	11	52	3	44	76
77	28	69	20	61	12	53	4	45

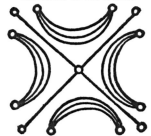

The same in Hebrew.

מה	ח	שדזלן	כט	ע	סככא	ין	מה
ו	מך	עטרחז	ל	עא	סאכב	יד	מך
מך	יה	רפ	פ	לא	עבכנ	זה	יה
נן	גן	חמהין	מאט	דכ	סרדכא	כל	נן
נן	כה	נז	ים	מצ	אכבלג	סח	כה
כך	סר	כז	נה	אב	עדכגמ	לך	סר
סך	לה	נסבכוז	נא	ב	מעאה	עה	לה
לו	עו	נבגחסרלן	א	גב	יאך	מך	עו
עו	מה	ר	נ	כמדוא	כל	יבסא	מה

Seal or Character of the Moon.

Character of the Spirit of the Moon.

Of the Spirit of the Spirits of the Moon.

Of the Intelligence of the Intelligences of the Moon.

NAMES ANSWERING TO THE NUMBERS OF SATURN.

♄

Numbers.	Divine Names.	Divine Names in Hebrew
3	Ab	אב
9	Hod	הד
15	Jah	יה
15	Hod	חוד
45	Jehovah extended	יורהאואוהא
45	Agiel, the Intelligence of Saturn	אניאל
45	Zazel, the Spirit of Saturn	זאזל

Names answering to the Numbers of Jupiter.

♃

4	Aba	אבא
16		הוה
16		אהי
34	El Ab	אלאב
136	Johphiel, the Intelligence of Jupiter	יהפיאל
136	Hismael, the Spirit of Jupiter	הסמאל

Names answering to the Numbers of Mars.

♂

Numbers.	Divine Names.	Divine Names in Hebrew
5	He, the letter of the holy name	ה
25		יהי
65	Adonai	אדני
325	Graphiel, the Intelligence of Mars	גראפיאל
325	Barzabel, the Spirit of Mars	ברצאבאל

Names answering to the Numbers of the Sun.

☉

6	Van, the letter of the holy name	ו
6	He extended, the letter of the holy name	הא
36	Eloh	אלה
111	Nachiel, the Intelligence of the Sun	נכיאל
666	Sorath, the Spirit of the Sun	סורת

Names answering to the Numbers of Venus.

♀

7	Aha	אהא
49	Hagiel, the Intelligence of Venus	הגיאל
175	Kedemel, the Spirit of Venus	קדמאל
1225	Bne Seraphim, the Intelligence of Venus	בני שרפים

Names answering to the Numbers of Mercury.

א

8	Asboga, eight extended	אזבוגה
64	Din	דין
64	Doni	דני
260	Tiriel, the Intelligence of Mercury	טיריאל
2080	Tapthartharath, the Spirit of Mercury	תפתרתרת

Names answering to the Numbers of the Moon.

ד

9	Hod	הד
81	Elim	אלים
369	Hasmodai, the Spirit of the Moon	השמודאי
3321	Schedbarschemoth Schartathan, the Spirit of the Spirits of the Moon	שדברשהמעהשרתתן
3321	Malcha betharsisim hed beruah schehalim, the Intelligence of the Intelligences of the Moon	קלכאבתרשיסימערברוחשההקים

Every natural virtue works things far more wonderful when it is not only compounded of a natural proportion, but also is informed by a choice observation of the celestials opportune to this (viz. when the celestial power is most strong to that effect which we desire, and also helped by many celestials), by subjecting inferiors to the celestials, as proper females, to be made fruitful by their males. Also, in every work there are to be observed the situation, motion and aspect of the stars and planets, in signs and degrees, and how all these stand in reference to the length and latitude of the climate; for by this are varied the qualities of the angles, which the rays of the celestial bodies upon the figure of the thing describe, according to which celestial virtues are infused. So when you are working anything which belongs to any planet, you must place it in its dignities fortunate, and powerful, and ruling in the day hour, and in the figure of the heavens. Neither must you expect the signification of the work to be powerful, but you must observe the Moon opportunely directed to this; for you shall do nothing without the assistance of the Moon. And if you have more patterns of your work, observe them all, being most powerful, and looking upon one another with a friendly aspect; and if you cannot have such aspects, it will be convenient at least that you take them angular. But you shall take the Moon either when she looks upon both, or is joined to one, and looks upon the other, or when she passes from hte conjunction or aspect of one, to the conjunction or aspect of the other; for that, I conceive, must in on wise be omitted. Also, you shall in every work observe Mercury, for he is a messenger between the higher gods and the infernal gods: when he goes to the good, he increases their goodness—when to the bad, he hath influence on their wickedness. We call it an unfortunate sign or planet, when it is, by the aspect of Saturn or Mars especially opposite or quadrant, for these are the aspects of enmity; but a conjunction, a trine, and a sextile aspect, are of friendship; between these there is a greater conjunction; but if you do not already behold it through a trine, and the planet be received, it is accounted as already conjoined. Now all planets are afraid of the conjunction of the Sun, rejoicing in the trine, and sextile aspect thereof.

Now we shall have the planets powerful when they are ruling in a house, or in exultation, or triplicity, or term, or face, without combustion of what is direct in the figure of the heavens, viz. when they are in angles, especially of the rising, or tenth, or in houses presently succeeding, or in their delights; but we must take heed that they are not in the bounds or under the dominion of Saturn or Mars, lest they be in dark degrees, in pits, or vacuities. You shall observe that the angles of the ascendant, and tenth, and seventh be fortunate; as also the lord of the ascendant, and place of the Sun and Moon, and place of the part of fortune, and the lord thereof, the lord of the foregoing conjunction and prevention. But that they of the malignant planet fall unfortunate; unless happily they be significators of thy work, or can be of any advantage to thee, or in thy revolution or birth they had the predominance, for then they are not at all to be depressed. Now we shall have the Moon powerful if she be in her house, or exaltation or triplicity, or face, or in degree convenient for the desired work; and if it had a mansion of these twenty-eight, suitable to itself and the work, let her not in the way be burnt up,* nor slow in course—let her not be in the eclipse, or burnt by the Sun, unless she be in unity with the Sun—let her not descend in the southern latitude, when she goeth out of the burning —neither let her be opposite to the Sun, nor deprived of light—let her not be hindered by Mars or Saturn.

There is the like consideration to be had in all things concerning the fixed stars. Know this, that all the fixed stars, are of the signification and nature of the seven planets; but some are of the nature of one planet, and some of two. Hence, as often as any planet is joined with any of the fixed stars of its own nature, the signification of that star is made more powerful, and the nature of the planet augmented; but if it be a star of two natures, the nature of that which shall be the stronger with it, shall overcome in signification: as for example, if it be of the nature of Mars and Venus, if Mars shall be the stronger with it, the nature of Mars shall overcome; but if Venus, the nature of Venus shall

---

* Via Combusta.

overcome. Now the natures of fixed stars are discovered by their colours, as they agree with certain planets and are ascribed to them. Now the colours of the planets are these:—of Saturn, blue, and leaden, and shining with this; of Jupiter, citrine, near to a paleness, and clear with this; of Mars, red and fiery; of the Sun, yellow, and when it rises red, afterwards glittering; of Venus, white and shining—white in the morning, and reddish in the evening; of Mercury, glittering; of the Moon, fair. Know, also, that of the fixed stars, by how much the greater, and brighter, and apparent they are, so much the greater and stronger is the signification: such are those stars called by the astrologers of the first and second magnitude. I will tell thee some of these which are more potent to this faculty, viz. the navel of Andromeda, in the twenty-second degree of Aries, of the nature of Venus and Mercury—some call it jovial and saturnine; the head of Algol, in the eighteenth degree of Taurus, of the nature of Saturn and Jupiter; the Pleiades are also in the twenty-second degree, a lunary star by nature, and complexion martial; also Aldeboram, in the third degree of Gemini, is of the nature of Mars, and complexion of Venus—but Adepts places this in the twenty-fifth degree of Aries; the Goat star, in the thirteenth degree of Gemini, is of the nature of Jupiter and Saturn; the Great Dog star is in the seventh degree of Cancer and Venereal; the Little Dog star is in the seventeenth degree of the same, and is of the nature of Mercury, and complexion of Mars; the King star, which is called the Heart of the Lion, is in the twenty-first degree of Leo, and of the nature of Jupiter and Mars; the tail of the Great Bear is in the nineteenth degree of Virgo, and is venereal and lunary. The star which is called the Right Wing of the Crow, is in the seventh degree of Libra; and in the thirteenth degree of the same, is the left wing of the same, and both of the nature of Saturn and Mars. The star called Spica, is in the sixteenth degree of the same, and is venereal and mercurial. In the seventeenth degree of the same is Alcameth, of the nature of Mars and Jupiter; but of this, when the Sun's aspect is full towards it—of that, when on the contrary. Elepheia, in the fourth degree of Scorpio, of the nature of Venus and Mars. The heart of the Scorpion is in the third degree of Sagittarius, of the nature of Mars and Jupiter. The falling Vulture is in the seventh degree of Capricorn, temperate, mercurial, and venereal. The tail of Capricorn is in the sixteenth degree of Aquarius, of the nature of Saturn and Mercury. The star called the Shoulder of the Horse, is in the third degree of Pisces, of the nature of Jupiter and Mars.—And it shall be a general rule for you to expect the proper gifts of the stars, whilst they rule—to be prevented of them, they being unfortunate, as is above shewed; for celestial bodies, inasmuch as they are affected fortunately or unfortunately, so much do they affect us, our works, and those things which we use, fortunately or unhappily. And although many effects proceed from the fixed stars, yet they are attributed to the planets; as because being more near to us, and more distinct and known, so because they execute whatever the superior stars communicate to them.

OF THE SUN AND MOON.

The Sun and Moon have obtained the administration of ruling the heavens, and all bodies under the heavens.   The Sun is the lord of all elementary virtues; and the Moon, by virtue of the Sun, is mistress of generation, increase or decrease.   By the Sun and Moon, life is infused into all things; which Orpheus calls the enlivening eyes of Heaven. The Sun giveth light to all things of itself, and gives it plentifully, not only to all things in heaven and air, but earth and deep.   Whatever good we have, Jamblicus says, we have it from the Sun alone; or from it through other things.   Hindus calls the Sun, the fountain of celestial light; and many of the Philosophers placed the soul of the world chiefly in the Sun, as that which, filling the whole globe of the Sun, doth send forth its rays on all sides, as it were a spirit through all things, distributing life, sense, and motion to the universe.   Hence the antient naturalists called the Sun the very heart of Heaven; and the Chaldeans put it as the middle of the Planets.   The Egyptians also placed it in the middle of the world, viz. between the two fives of the world; i. e., above the Sun they place five planets, and under him, the Moon and four elements. For it is, amongst the other stars, the image and statue of the great Prince of both worlds, viz. terrestial and celestial; the true light, and the most exact image of God himself: whose essence resembles the Father—light, the Son—heat, the Holy Ghost.   So that the Platonists have nothing to hold forth the divine essence more manifestly by than this. The Sun disposes even the very spirit and mind of man, which Homer says, and is approved by Aristotle, that there are in the mind such like motions as the Sun, the prince and moderator of the planets, brings to us every day; but the Moon, the nearest to the earth, the receptacle of all the heavenly influences, by the swiftness of her course, is joined to the Sun, and the other planets and stars, every month; and receiving the beams and influences of all the other planets and stars, as a conception, bringing them forth to the inferior world, as being next to itself; for all the stars have influence on it, being the last receiver, which afterwards communicates the influence of all the superiors to these inferiors, and pours them forth on the earth; and it more manifestly disposes these inferiors than others.   Therefore her motion is to be observed before the others, as the parent of all conceptions, which it diversely issues forth in these inferiors, according to the diverse complexion, motion, situation, and different aspects to the planets and other stars; and though it receives powers from all the stars, yet especially from the

Sun, as oft as it is in conjunction with the same, it is replenished with vivifying virtue; and, according to the aspect thereof, it borrows its complexion. From it the heavenly bodies begin that series of things which Hindus calls the golden chain; by which every thing and cause, being linked one to another, do depend on the superior even until it may be brought unto the supreme cause of all, from which all things depend; hence it is, that, without the Moon intermediating, we cannot at any time attract the power of the superiors; therefore, to obtain the virtue of any star, take the stone and herb of that planet, when the Moon fortunately comes under, or has a good aspect on, that star.

And seeing the Moon measures the whole space of the Zodiac in the time of twenty-eight days, hence it is that the wise men of the *Indians,* and most of the ancient astrologers have granted twenty-eight mansions to the Moon, which, being fixed in the eighth sphere, do enjoy divers names and properties, from the various signs and stars which are contained in them; through which, while the Moon wanders, it obtains many other powers and virtues; but every one of these mansions, according to the opinion of *Athumech,* or *Alcheymech;* that is, the spike of Virgo, or flying spike: *Abraham,* contained twelve degrees, and fifty-one minutes, and almost twenty-six seconds, whose names, and also their beginnings in the Zodiac, of the eighth sphere, are these:—The first is called *Alnath;* that is, the horns of Aries: his beginning is from the head of Aries, of the eighth sphere: it causes discords and journies. The second is called *Allothaim, or Albochan;* that is, the belly of Aries; and his beginning is from the twelfth degree of the same sign, fifty-one minutes, twenty-two seconds complete: it conduces to the finding of treasures, and to the retaining captives. The third is called *Achaomazon,* or *Athoray;* that is, showing, or Pleiades: his beginning is from the twenty-fifth degree of Aries complete, forty-two minutes, and fifty-one seconds; it is profitable to sailors, huntsmen and alchymists. The fourth mansion is called *Aldebaram,* or *Aldelamen;* that is, the eye or head of Taurus: his beginning is from the eighth degree of Taurus, thirty-four minutes and seventeen seconds of the same, Taurus being excluded: it causes the destruction and hindrances of buildings, fountains, wells, gold mines, the flight of creeping things, and begets discord. The fifth is called *Alchatay,* or *Albachay;* the beginning of it is after the twenty-first degree of Taurus, twenty-five minutes, forty seconds: it helps to the return from a journey, to the instruction of scholars; it confirms edifices, it gives health and good-will. The sixth is called *Athanna,* or *Alchaya;* that is, the little star of great light: his beginning is after the fourth degree of Gemini, seventeen minutes, and nine seconds; it conduces to hunting and besieging towns, and revenge of princes: it destroys harvest and fruits, and hinders the operation of the physician. The seventh is called *Aldimiach,* or *Alarzach;* that is, the arm of Gemini, and begins from the seventeenth degree of Gemini, eight minutes, and thirty-four seconds, and lasts even to the end of the sign; it confirms gain and friendship; it is profitable to lovers, and destroys magistracies: and so is one quarter of the heaven completed in these seven mansions, and in the like order and number of degrees, minutes, and seconds; the remaining mansions, in every quarter, have their several beginnings; namely, so that in the first sign of this quarter three mansions take their beginnings; in the other two signs, two mansions in each; therefore the seven following mansions begin with Cancer, whose names are *Alnaza, Anatrachya;* that is, misty or cloudy, viz. the eighth mansion; it causes love, friendship, and society of fellow travellers: it drives away mice, and afflicts captives, confirming their imprisonment. After this is the ninth, called *Archaam,* or *Arcaph;* that is the eye of the Lion: it hinders harvest and travellers, and puts discord between men. The tenth is called *Algelioche,* or *Albgebh;* that is the neck or forehead of Leo: it strengthens buildings, promotes love, benevolence, and help against enemies. The eleventh is called *Azobra,* or *Ardaf;* that is, the hair of the lion's head: it is good for voyages, and gain by merchandise, and for redemption of captives. The twelfth is called *Alzarpha,* or *Azarpha;* that is the tail of Leo: it gives prosperity to harvest and plantations, but hinders seamen; and is good for the bettering of servants, captives, and companions. The thirteenth is named *Alhaire;* that is, Dog stars, or the wings of Virgo: it is prevalent for benevolence, gain, voyages, harvest, and freedom of captives. The fourteenth is called *Achureth,* or *Arimet;* by others, *Azimeth,* it causes the love of married folks; it cures the sick, is profitable to sailors, but hinders journies by lands; and in these the second quarter of the heaven is completed. The other seven follow: the first of which begins in the head of Libra, viz. the fifteenth mansion, and its name is *Agrapha,* or *Algrapha;* that is, covered, or covered flying: it is profitable for extracting treasures, for digging of pits, it assists divorce, discord, and destruction of houses and enemies, and hinders travellers. The sixteenth is called *Azubene,* or *Ahubene;* that is, the horns of Scorpio: it hinders journies and wedlock, harvest and merchandise: it prevails for redemption of captives. The seventeenth is called *Alchil;* that is, the crown of Scorpio: it betters a bad fortune, makes love durable, strengthens buildings, and helps seamen. The eighteenth is called *Alchas,* or *Altob;* that is, the heart of Scorpio: it causes discord, sedition, conspiracy against princes and mighty ones, and revenge from enemies; but it frees captives, and helps edifices. The nineteenth is called *Allatha,* or *Achata;* by others, *Hycula,* or *Axala;* that is, the tail of Scorpio: it helps in besieging of cities, and taking of towns, and in the driving of men from their places, and for the destruction of seamen and perdition of captives. The twentieth is called *Abnahaya;* that is, a beam: it helps for the taming of wild beasts, for strengthening

Geomantic Characters.

of prisons; it destroys the wealth of societies; it compels a man to come to a certain place. The twenty-first is called *Abeda,* or *Albeldach,* which is a desert: it is good for harvest, gain, buildings, and travellers, and causes divorce; and in this is the third quarter of heaven completed. There remains the seven last mansions completing the last quarter of Heaven: the first of which, being in order to the twenty-second, beginning from the head of Capricorn, called *Sadahacha,* or *Zodeboluch,* or *Zandeldena;* that is, a pastor: it promotes the flight of servants and captives, that they may escape; and helps the curing of disease. The twenty-third is called *Zababola,* or *Zobrach;* that is, swallowing: it is for divorce, liberty of captives and health to the sick. The twenty-fourth is called *Sadabath,* or *Chadezoad;* that is, the star of fortune: it is prevalent for the benevolence of married people, for the victory of soldiers; it hurts the execution of government, and prevents its being exercised. The twenty-fifth is called *Sadalabra,* or *Sadalachia;* that is, a butterfly, or a spreading forth: it favours besieging and revenge; it destroys enemies, and causes divorce; confirms prisons and buildings, hastens messengers; it conduces to spells against copulation and so binds every member of man that it cannot perform its duty. The twenty-sixth is called *Alpharg,* or *Phragal Mocaden;* that is, the first drawing: it causes union, health of captives, destroys buildings and prisons. The twenty-seventh is called *Alchara, Alyhalgalmoad,* or the second drawing: it increases harvests, revenues, gain, and heals infirmities, but hinders buildings, prolongs prisons, causes danger to seamen, and helps to infer mischiefs on whom you shall please. The twenty-eighth and last is called *Albotham,* or *Alchalcy;* that is, Pisces; it increases harvest and merchandise; it secures travellers through dangerous places; it makes for the joy of married people; but it strengthens prisons, and causes loss of treasures. And in these twenty-eight mansions lie hid many secrets of the wisdom of the antients, by which they wrought wonders on all things which are under the circle of the Moon; and they attributed to every mansion his resemblances, images, and seals, and his president intelligences, and worked by the virtue of them after different manners.

So great is the extent, power, and efficacy of the celestial bodies, that not only natural things, but also artificial, when they are rightly exposed to those above, do presently suffer by that most potent agent, and obtain a wonderful life. The magicians affirm, that not only by the mixture and application of natural things, but also in images, seals, rings, glasses, and some other instruments, being opportunately framed under a certain constellation, some celestial illustrations may be taken, and some wonderful thing may be received; for the beams of the celestial bodies being animated, living, sensual, and bringing along with them admirable gifts, and a most violent power, do, even in a moment, and at the first touch, imprint wonderful powers in the images, though their matter be less capable. Yet they bestow more powerful virtues on the images if they be framed not of any, but of a certain matter, namely, whose natural, but also specifical virtue is agreeable with the work, and the figure of the image is like to the celestial; for such an image, both in regard to the matter naturally congruous to the operation and celestial influence, and also for its figure being like to the heavenly one, is best prepared to receive the operations and powers of the celestial bodies and figures, and instantly receives the heavenly gift into itself; though it constantly worketh on another thing, and other things yield obedience to it.

IMAGES OF THE ZODIAC.

But the celestial images, according to whose likeness images of this kind are framed, are many in the heavens; some visible and conspicuous, others only imaginary, conceived and set down by the Adepts and Master Lamas; and their parts are so ordered, that even the figures of some of them are distinguished from others; for this reason they place in the circle of the Zodiac twelve general images, according to the number of the signs; of these, they constituting Aries, Leo, and Sagittarius, for the fiery and oriental triplicity, report that it is profitable against fevers, palsy, dropsy, gout, and all cold and phlegmatic infirmities; and that it makes him who carries it to be acceptable, eloquent, ingenious and honourable; because they are the houses of Mars, Sol, and Jupiter. Make, also, the image of a lion against melancholy, phantasies, dropsy, plague and fevers, and to expel diseases; at the hour of the Sun, the first degree of the sign Leo ascending, which is the face and decanate of Jupiter; but against the stone, and diseases of the reins, and against hurts of beasts, they made the same image when Sol, in the heart of the lion, obtained the midst of heaven. And again, because Gemini, Libra, and Aquarius, do constitute the ærial and occidental triplicity, and are the houses of Mercury, Venus, and Saturn, they I say do put to flight diseases, to conduce to friendship and concord, to prevail against melancholy, and to cause health; and I do report that Aquarius especially frees from the quartan. Also, that Cancer, Scorpio, and Pisces, because they constitute the watery and northern triplicity, do prevail against hot and dry fevers, also against the hectic, and all choleric passions; but Scorpio, because among the members it respects the privy parts, doth provoke to lust; but these did frame it for this purpose, his third face ascending, which belongs to Venus; and make the same, against serpents and scorpions, poisons and evil spirits, his second face ascending, which is the face of the Sun, and decanate of Jupiter; this maketh him who carries it wise, of a good colour; and the image of Cancer is most efficacious against serpents and poison, when Sol and Luna are in conjunction in it, and ascend in the first and third face; for this is the face of Venus, and the decanate of Luna; but the second face of Luna the decanate of Jupiter. Serpents are tormented when the Sun is in Cancer; also, that Taurus, Virgo, and Capricorn, because they constitute the earthly and southern triplicity, do cure hot infirmities, and prevail against the synocal fever; it makes those who carry it grateful, acceptable, eloquent, devout and religious; because they are the houses of Venus, Mars, and Saturn. Capricorn also is certain to keep men in safety, and also places in security, because it is the exaltation of Mars.

IMAGES OF THE PLANETS.

But now what images should you attribute to the planets. Although of these things very large volumes have been written by the antient wise men, so that there is no need to declare them here, notwithstanding I will recite a few of them; for the operations of Saturn, *Saturn* ascending in a stone, which is called the load-stone, make the image of a man, having the countenance of a hart, and camel's feet, and sitting upon a chair or else a dragon, holding in his right hand a scythe, in his left a dart, which image will be profitable for prolongation of life; for Adepts, in their teachings, prove that Saturn conduces to the prolongation of life; where, also, they prove that certain regions of India being subject to Saturn, there men are of a very long life, and die not unless by extreme old age. They make, also, an image of Saturn, for length of days, in a sapphire, at the hour of Saturn, *Saturn* ascending or fortunately constituted: whose figure was an old man sitting upon a high chair, having his hands lifted above his head, and in them holding a fish or sickle, and under his feet a bunch of grapes, his head covered with a black or dusky coloured cloth, and all his garments black or dark. Also make this same image against the stone, and diseases of the kidnies, viz. in the hour of Saturn, *Saturn* ascending with the third face of Aquarius. Make also, from the operations of Saturn, an image for the increasing of power, Saturn ascending in Capricorn; the form of which was an old man leaning on a staff, having in his hand a crooked sickle, and clothed in black. Make an image of melted copper, Saturn ascending in his rising, viz. in the first degree of Aries, or the first degree of Capricorn; which image I affirm to speak with a man's voice. Make also, from the operations of Saturn and also Mercury, an image of cast metal, like a beautiful man, which will assist you to foretell things to come; and make it on the day of Mercury, on the third hour of Saturn, the sign of Gemini ascending, being the house of Mercury, signifying prophets; Saturn and Mercury being in conjunction in Aquarius, in the ninth house of heaven, which is also called God. Moreover, let Saturn have a trine aspect on the ascendant, and the Moon in like manner, and the Sun have an aspect on the place of conjunction;

Venus, obtaining some angle may be powerful and occidental; let Mars be combust by the Sun, but let it not have an aspect of Saturn and Mercury; for I say that the splendour of the powers of these stars was diffused upon this image, and it did speak with men, and declare those things which are profitable for them.

From the operations of Jupiter make, for the prolongation of life, an image in the hour of Jupiter, Jupiter being in his exaltation fortunately ascending, in a clear and white stone; whose figure was a man crowned clothed with garments of a saffron colour, riding upon an eagle or dragon, having in his right hand a dart, about, as it were, to strike it into the head of the same eagle or dragon. Make, also, another image of Jupiter, at the same convenient season, in a white and clear stone, especially in crystal; and it was a naked man crowned, having both his hands joined together and lifted up, as it were, depreciating something sitting in a four-footed chair, which is carried by four winged boys; and I affirm that this image increases felicity, riches, honours, and confers benevolence and prosperity, and frees from enemies. Make, also, another image of Jupiter, for a religious and glorious life, and advancement of fortune; whose figure is a man having the head of a lion or a ram, and eagle's feet, and clothed in saffron coloured clothes.

For the operations of Mars, make an image in the hour of Mars (Mars ascending in the second face of Aries), in a martial stone, especially in a diamond; the form of which was a man armed, riding upon a lion, having in his right hand a naked sword erect, carrying in his left hand the head of a man. I report that an image of this kind renders a man powerful in good and evil, so that he shall be feared by all; and whoever carries it, they give him the power of enchantment, so that he shall terrify men by his looks when he is angry, and stupify them. Make another image of Mars, for obtaining boldness, courage, and good fortune, in wars and contentions; the form of which was a soldier, armed and crowned, girt with a sword, carrying in his right hand a long lance; and they made this at the hour of Mars, the first face of Scorpio ascending with it.

From the operations of the Sun make thee an image at the hour of the Sun, the first face of Leo ascending with the Sun; the form of which was a king crowned, sitting in a chair, having a raven in his bosom, and under his feet a globe: he is clothed in saffron coloured clothes. This image renders men invincible and honourable, and helps to bring their business to a good end, and to drive away vain dreams; also to be prevalent against fevers, and the plague; and they made it in a balanite stone, or a ruby, at the hour of the Sun, when he is in his exaltation, fortunately ascends. Make another image of the Sun in a diamond, at the hour of the Sun ascending in his exaltation; the figure of which is a woman crowned, with the gesture of one, dancing and laughing, standing in a chariot drawn by four horses, having in her right hand a looking-glass or buckler, in the left a staff, leaning on her breast, carrying a flame of fire on her head. This image renders a man fortunate, and rich, and beloved of all; and they made this image on a cornelian stone, at the hour of the Sun ascending in the first face of Leo, against lunatic passions, which proceed from the combustion of the Moon.

From the operations of Venus make thee an image, which was available for favour and benevolence, at the very hour it ascended into Pisces; the form of which is the image of a woman, having the head of a bird, the feet of an eagle, and holding a dart in her hand. Make another image of Venus, to obtain the love of women, in the lapis lazuli, at the hour of Venus, *Venus* ascending in *Taurus;* the figure of which is a naked maid, with her hair spread abroad, having a looking-glass in her hand, and a chain tied about her neck—and near her a handsome young man, holding her with his left hand by the chain, but with his right hand doing up her hair, and both looking lovingly on one another—and about them is a little winged boy, holding a sword or dart. Make another image of Venus, the first face of *Taurus, Libra,* or *Pisces,* ascending with Venus; the figure of which was a little maid, with her hair spread abroad, clothed in long and white garments, holding a laurel apple, or flowers, in her right hand, in her left a comb: it is said to make men pleasant, jocund, strong, cheerful and to give beauty.

For the operations of *Mercury* make an image of *Mercury, Mercury* ascending in *Gemini;* the form of which was a handsome young man, bearded, having in his left hand a rod, round which a serpent was entwined—in the right he carries a dart; having his feet winged. This image confers knowledge, eloquence, diligence in merchandise, and gain; moreover, to obtain peace and concord, and cure fevers. Make another image of Mercury, ascending in Virgo, for good will, wit, and memory; the form of which is a man sitting upon a chair, or riding on a peacock, having eagle's feet, and on his head a crest, and in his left hand holding a cock of fire.

For the operations of the Moon make thee an image for travellers against weariness, at the hour of the Moon, the *Moon* ascending in its exaltation; the figures of which is a man leaning on a staff, having a bird on his head, and a flourishing tree before him. Make another image of the Moon for the increase of the fruits of the earth, and against poisons, and infirmities of children, at the hour of the Moon, it ascending in the first of Cancer, the figure of which is a woman cornuted, riding on a bull, or a dragon with seven heads or a crab, and she hath in her right hand a dart, in her left a looking-glass, clothed with white or green, and having on her head two serpents with horns twihed together, and to each arm a serpent twined about, and to each foot one in like manner. And thus much is spoken concerning the figures of the planets, may suffice.

Make, also, the image of the head and tail of the Dragon of the Moon, namely, between an ærial and fiery circle, the likeness of a serpent, with the head of a hawk, tied about them after the manner of the great letter Theta; they made it when Jupiter, with the head, obtained the mid heaven; which image I affirm to avail much for the success of petitions, and would signify by this image a good and fortunate genius, which they would represent by this image of the serpent; for the Hindu Adepts and Yoghees do extol this creature above all others, and say it is a divine creature, and hath a divine nature; for in this is a more acute spirit, and a greater fire than in any other, which thing is manifest both by his swift motion without feet, hands, or any other instruments; and also that it often renews its age with his skin, and becomes young again; but they made the image of the tail like as when the Moon was eclipsed in the tail, or ill affected by Saturn or Mars, and they made it to introduce anguish, infirmity, and Misfortune: we call it an evil genius.

Make, also, images for every mansion of the Moon as follows:—

In the first, for the destruction of some one, make, in an iron ring, the image of a black man, in a garment of hair, and girdled round, casting a small lance with his right hand: seal this in black wax, and perfume it with liquid storax, and wish evil to come.

In the second, against the wrath of the prince, and for reconciliation with him, seal, in white wax and mastich, the image of a king crowned, and perfumed it with lignum aloes.

In the third, make an image in a silver ring, whose table was square; the figure of which was a woman, well clothed, sitting in a chair, her right hand being lifted up on her head; they sealed it, and perfumed it with musk, camphire, and calamus aromaticus. I affirmed that this gives happy fortune, and every good thing.

In the fourth, for revenge, separation, enmity, and ill-will, seal, in red wax, the image of a soldier sitting on a horse, holding a serpent in his right hand: perfume it with red myrrh and storax.

In the fifth, for the favour of kings and officers, and good entertainment, seal, in silver, the head of a man, and perfumed it with red sanders.

In the sixth, to procure love between two, seal, in white wax, two images, embracing one another, and perfumed them with lignum aloes and amber.

In the seventh, to obtain every good thing, seal, in silver, the image of a man, well clothed, holding up his hands to Heaven, as it were, praying and supplicating, and perfumed it with good odours.

In the eighth, for victory in war, make a seal in tin, being an image of an eagle, having the face of a man, and perfume it with brimestone.

In the ninth, to cause infirmities, make a seal of lead, being the image of a man wanting his privy parts, covering his eyes with his hands; and perfume it with rosin of the pine.

In the tenth, to facilitate child bearing, and to cure the sick, make a seal of gold, being the head of a lion, and perfume it with amber.

In the eleventh, for fear, reverence, and worship, make a seal of a plate of gold, being the image of a man riding on a lion, holding the ear thereof in his left hand, and in his right holding forth a bracelet of gold; and they perfume it with good odours and saffron.

In the twelfth, for the separation of lovers, make a seal of black lead, being the image of a dragon, fighting with a man; and perfume it with the hairs of a lion, and assafœtida.

In the thirteenth, for the agreement of married people, and for dissolving of all the charms against copulation, make a seal of the images of both (of the man in red wax, and the woman in white), and caused them to embrace one another, perfuming it with lignum aloes and amber.

In the fourteenth, for divorce and separation of the man from the woman, make a seal of red copper, being the image of a dog biting his tail; and then perfume it with the hair of a black dog and a black cat.

In the fifteenth, to obtain friendship and good will, make the image of a man sitting, and inditing letters, and perfumed it with frankincense and nutmegs.

In the sixteenth, for gaining much merchandizing, make a seal of silver, being the image of a man, sitting on a chair, holding a balance in his hand; and they perfume it with well smelling spices.

In the seventeenth, against thieves and robbers, seal with an iron seal the image of an ape, and perfume it with the air of an ape.

In the eighteenth, against fevers and pains of the belly, make a seal of copper, being the image of a snake with his tail above his head; and perfume it with hartshorn; and this same seal put to flight serpents, and all venemous creatures, from the place where it is buried.

In the nineteenth, for facilitating birth, and provoking the menstrues, make a seal of copper, being the image of a woman holding her hands upon her face; and perfume it with liquid storax.

In the twentieth, for hunting, make a seal of tin, being the image of Sagittary, half a man and half a horse; and perfume it with the head of a wolf.

In the twenty-first, for the destruction of some body, make the image of a man, with a double countenance before and behind; and perfume it with brimstone and jet, and put it in a box of brass, and with it brimstone and jet, and the hair of him whom they would hurt.

In the twenty-second, for the security of runaways, make a seal of iron, being the image of a man, with wings on his feet, bearing a helmet on his head; and perfume it with *argent vive*.

In the twenty-third, for destruction and wasting, make a seal of iron, being the image of a cat, having a dog's head; and perfume it with dog's hair taken from the head, and buried it in the place where they intended the hurt.

In the twenty-fourth, for multiplying herds of cattle, take the horn of a ram, bull, or goat, or of that sort of cattle you would increase, and seal in it, burning, with an iron seal, the image of a woman giving suck to her son; and hang it on the neck of that cattle who are the leader of the flock, or seal it in his horn.

In the twenty-fifth, for the preservation of trees and harvest, seal in the wood of a fig tree, the image of a man planting; and perfume it with the flowers of the fig tree, and hang it on the tree.

In the twenty-sixth, for love and favour, seal, in white wax and mastich, the figure of a woman washing and combing her hair; and perfume it with good odours.

In the twenty-seventh, to destroy fountains, pits, medicinal waters, and baths, make, of red earth, the image of a man winged, holding in his hand an empty vessel, and perforated; and the image being burnt, and put in the vessel assafœtida and liquid storax, and bury it in the pond or fountain which you would destroy.

In the twenty-eighth, for getting fish together, make a seal of copper, being the image of a fish; and perfume it with the skin of a sea fish, and cast it into the water where you would have the fish gathered.

Moreover, together with the aforesaid images, write down also the names of the spirits, and their characters, and invoke and pray for those things which you desire to obtain.

MAGIC SEALS.

The celestial souls send forth their virtues to the celestial bodies, which transmit them to this sensible world; for the virtues of the terrene orb proceed from no other cause than celestial. Hence the Adepts, that will work by them, uses a cunning invocation of the superiors, with mysterious words and a certain kind of ingenious speech, drawing the one to the other; yet by a natural force, through a certain mutual agreement between them, whereby things follow of their own accord, or sometimes are drawn unwillingly. Hence I say, "that when any one, by binding or bewitching, calls upon the Sun or other stars, praying them to assist the work desired, the Sun and other stars do not hear his words; but are moved, after a certain manner, by a certain conjunction and mutual series, whereby the parts of the world are mutually subordinate

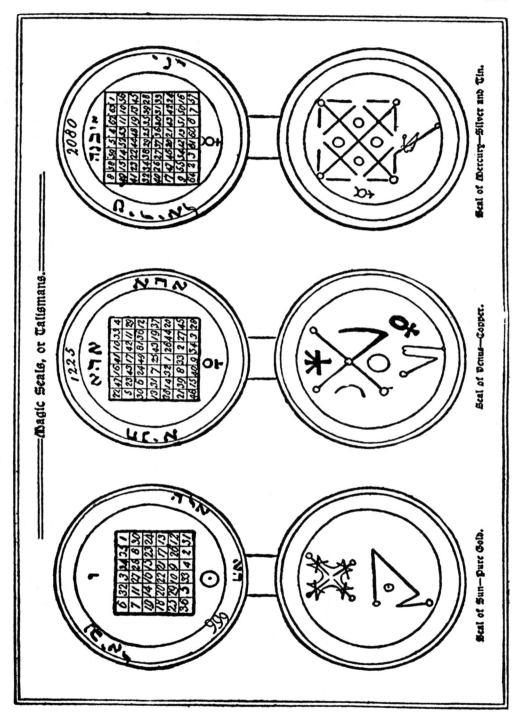

Magic Seals, or Talismans.

Seal of Mercury—Silver and Tin.

Seal of Venus—Copper.

Seal of Sun—Pure Gold.

the one to the other, and have a mutual consent, by reason of their great union: as in a man's body, one member is moved by perceiving the motion of another; and in a harp, one string is moved by the motion of another. So when any one moves any part of the world, other parts are moved by the perceiving of that motion."—The knowledge, therefore, of the dependency of things following one the other, is the foundation of all wonderful operation, which is necessarily required to the exercising the power of attracting superior virtues. Now the words of men are certain natural things; and because the parts of the world mutually draw one the other; therefore an Adept invocating by words, works by powers fitted to Nature, by leading some by love of the one to the other; or drawing others, by reason of the one following after the other; or by repelling, by reason of the enmity of one to the other, from the contrariety and difference of things, and multitude of virtues; which, although they are contrary and different, yet perfect one part. Sometimes, also, he compels things by way of authority, by the celestial virtue, because he is not a stranger to the heavens. A man, therefore, if he receives the impression of a ligation, or fascination, doth not receive it according to the rational soul, but sensual; and if he suffers in any part, he suffers according to the animal part; for they cannot draw a knowing and intelligent man by reason, but by receiving that impression and force by sense; inasmuch as the animal spirit of man is, by the influence of the celestials, and co-operation of the things of the world, affected beyond his former and natural disposition. As the son moves the father to labour, although unwilling to keep and maintain him, although he be wearied; and the desire to rule, is moved by anger and other labours to get the dominion; and the indigency of nature, and fear of poverty, moves a man to desire riches; and the ornaments and beauty of women, is an incitement to concupiscence; and the harmony of a wise musician moves his hearers with various passions, whereof some do voluntary follow the consonancy of art, others conform themselves by gesture, although unwilling, because their sense is captivated, their reason not being intent to these things. Hence they fall into errors, who think those things to be above nature, or contrary to nature—which indeed are by nature, and according to nature. We must know, therefore, that every superior moves its next inferior, in its degree and order, not only in bodies, but also in spirits: so the universal soul moves the particular soul; the rational acts upon the sensual, and that upon the vegetable; and every part of the world acts upon another, and every part is apt to be moved by another. And every part of this inferior world suffers from the heavens, according to their nature and aptitude, as one part of the animal body suffers for another. And the superior intellectual world moves all things below itself; and, after a manner, contains all the same beings, from the first to the last, which are in the inferior world. Celestial bodies, therefore, move the bodies of the elementary world, compounded, generable, sensible (from the circumference to the centre), by superior, perpetual, and spiritual essences, depending on the primary intellect, which is the acting intellect; but upon the virtue put in by the word of God; which word the wise Hindu Adepts call, the Cause of Causes; because from it are produced all beings: the acting intellect, which is the second, from it depends; and that by reason of the union of the word with the First Author, from whom all things being are truly produced: the word, therefore, is the image of God—the acting intellect, the image of the word—the soul is the image of this intellect—and our word is the image of the soul; by which it acts upon natural things, naturally, because nature is the work thereof. And every one of those perfects his subsequent: as a father his son; and none of the latter exists without the formei; for they are depending among themselves by a kind of ordinate dependency —so that when the latter is corrupted, it is returned into that which was next before it, until it comes to the heavens; then to the universal soul; and, lastly, into the acting intellect, by which all other creatures exist; and itself exists in the principal author, which is the creating word of God, to which, at length, all things are returned. Our soul, therefore, if it will work any wonderful thing in these inferiors, must have respect to their beginning, that it may be strengthened and illustrated by that, and receive power of acting through each degree, from the very first Author. Therefore we must be more diligent in contemplating the souls of the stars—then their bodies, and the super-celestial and intellectual world—then the celestial, corporeal, because that is more noble; although, also, this be excellent, and the way to that, and without which medium the influence of the superior cannot be attained to. As for example: the Sun is the king of stars, most full of light; but receives it from the intelligible world, above all other stars, because the soul thereof is more capable of intelligible splendour. Wherefore he that desires to attract the influence of the Sun must contemplate upon the Sun; not only by the speculation of the exterior light, but also of the interior. And no man can do this, unless he return to the soul of the Sun, and become like to it, and comprehend the intelligible light thereof with an intellectual sight, as the sensible light with the corporeal eye; for this man shall be filled with the light thereof, and the light whereof, which is an under type impressed by the supernal orb, it receives into itself; with the illustration whereof his intellect being endowed, and truly like to it, and being assisted by it, shall at length attain to that supreme brightness, and to all forms that partake thereof; and when he hath received the light of the supreme degree, then his soul shall come to perfection, and be made like to spirits of the Sun, and shall attain to the virtues and illustrations of the supernatural virtue, and shall enjoy the power of them, if he has obtained faith in the First Author. In the first place, therefore, we must implore assistance from the First Author; and praying, not only with mouth, but a religious gesture and supplicant soul, also, abundantly, incessantly, and sincerely, that he would enlighten our mind, and remove darkness, growing upon our souls by reason of our bodies.

KEY TO TALISMANIC MAGIC.

I will now shew thee the observations of celestial bodies, which are required for the practice of these things, which are briefly as follows:—
To make any one fortunate, make an image at that time in which the *significator of life, the giver of life,* or *Hylech the signs and planets,* are fortunate: let the ascendant and mid-heaven, and the lords thereof be fortunate; and also, the place of the Sun and Moon; part of fortune and lord of conjunction or prevention, make before their nativity, by depressing the malignant planets, *i. e.,* taking the times when they are depressed. But if you would make an image to procure misery, you must do contrary to this; and those which you placed fortunate, you must now make unfortunate, by taking the malignant stars when they rule. And the same means you must take to make any place, region, city, or house unfortunate. But if you would make any one unfortunate who hath injured you, let there be an image made under the ascension of that man whom thou wouldst make unfortunate; and thou shalt take, when unfortunate, the lord of the house of his life, the lord of the ascendant and the Moon, the lord of the house of the Moon, the lord of the house of the lord ascending, and the tenth house and the lord thereof. Now, for the building, success, or fitting of any place, place fortunes in the ascendant thereof; and in the first and tenth, the second and eighth house, thou shalt make the lord of the ascendant, and the lord of the house of the Moon, fortunate. But to chase away certain animals (from any place) that are noxious to thee, that they may not generate or abide there, make an image under the ascension of that animal which thou wouldst chase away or destroy, and after the likeness thereof; for instance, now, suppose thou wouldst wish to chase away scorpions from any place; let an image of a scorpion be made, the sign Scorpio ascending with the Moon; then thou shalt make unfortunate the ascendant, and the lord thereof, and the lord of the house of *Mars;* and thou shalt make unfortunate the lord of the ascendant in the eighth house; and let them be joined with an aspect malignant, as opposite or square, and write upon the image the name of the ascendant, and of the lord thereof, and the Moon, the lord of the day and hour; and let there be a pit made in the middle of the place from which thou wouldst drive them, and put into it some earth taken out of the four corners of the same place, then bury the image there, with the head downwards,

saying—*"This is the burying of the Scorpions, that they may be forced to leave, and come no more into this place."—And so do by the rest.*

Now for gain, make an image under the ascendant of that man to whom thou wouldst appoint the gain; and thou shalt make the lord of the second house, which is the house of substance, to be joined with the lord of the ascendant, in a trine or sextile aspect, and let there be a reception amongst them; thou shalt make fortunate the eleventh, and the lord thereof, and eighth; and, if thou canst, put part of fortune in the ascendant or second; and let the image be buried in that place, or from that place, to which thou wouldst appoint the gain or fortune. Likewise, for agreement or love, let be made an image in the day of Jupiter, under the ascendant of the nativity of him whom you would wish to be beloved; make fortunate the ascendant and the tenth, and hide the evil from the ascendant; and you must have the lords of the tenth, and planets of the eleventh, fortunate, joined in the lord of the ascendant, from the trine or sextile, with reception; then proceed to make another image, for him whom thou would stir up to love; whether it be a friend, or female, or brother, or relation, or companion of him whom thou would have favoured or beloved, if so, make an image under the ascension of the eleventh house from the ascendant of the first image; but if the party be a wife, or a husband, let it be made under the ascension of the seventh; if a brother, sister, or cousin, under the ascension of the third house; if a mother, of a tenth, and so on:—now let the significator of the ascendant of the second image be joined to the significator of the ascendant of the first, and let there be between them a reception, and let the rest be fortunate, as in the first image; afterwards join both the images together in a mutual embrace, or put the face of the second to the back of the first, and let them be wrapped up in silk, and cast away or spoiled.

Also, for the success of petitions, and obtaining of a thing denied, or taken, or possessed by another, make an image under the ascendant of him who petitions for the thing; and cause the lord of the second house to be joined with the lord of the ascendant, from a trine or sextile aspect, and let there be a reception betwixt them; and, if it can be so, let the lord of the second be in the obeying signs, and the lord of ascendant in the ruling; make fortunate the ascendant and the lord thereof; and beware that the lord of the ascendant be not retrograde, or combust, or cadent, or in the house opposition, *i. e.,* in the seventh from his own house; let him not be hindered by the malignant planets, but let him be strong and in an angle; thou shalt make fortunate the ascendant, and the lord of the second, and the Moon: and make another image for him that is petitioned to, and begin it under the ascendant belonging to him: as if he is a king, or prince, &c., begin it under the ascendant of the tenth house from the ascendant of the first image; if a father, under the fourth; if a son, under the fifth, and so of the like; then put the significator of the second image, joined with the lord of the ascendant of the first image from a trine or sextile, and let him receive it; and put them both strong and fortunate, without any hindrance; make all evil fall from them; thou shalt make fortunate the tenth and the fourth, if thou canst, or any of them; and when the second image shall be perfect, join it with the first, face to face, and wrap them in clean linen, and bury them in the middle of his house who is the petitioner, under a fortunate significator, *the fortune being strong;* and let the face of the first image be towards the north, or rather towards that place where the thing petitioned for doth remain; or, if it happens that the petitioner goes forward to obtain the thing desired or petitioned for, let him carry the said images with him.   Thus I have given, in examples, the key of all Talismanical operations whatsoever, by which wonderful effects may be wrought either by images, by rings, by glasses, by seals, by tables, or any other magical instruments whatsoever; but as these have their chief grounds in the true knowledge of the effects of the planets, and the rising of the constellations, I recommend an earnest attention to that part of Astrology which teaches of the power, influences and effects of the celestial bodies amongst th mselves generally; likewise, I would recommend the disciple to be expe : in the aspect, motions, declinations; risings, &c., &c., of the seven planets, and perfectly to understand their natures, either mixed or simple; also, to be ready and correct in the erecting of a figure, at any time, to shew the true position of the heavens; there being so great a sympathy between the celestials and ourselves; and to observe all the other rules which we have plentifully recited: and, without doubt, the industrious student shall receive the satisfaction of bringing his operations and experiments to effect that which he ardently desires.   With which, wishing all success to the contemplator of the creature and the Creator, I will here close up this part of my work, and the conclusion of my chapter on Talismanical Magic.

This is the end of this publication.

Any remaining blank pages are for our book binding
requirements and are blank on purpose.

To search thousands of interesting publications like this one,
please remember to visit our website at:

http://www.kessinger.net

CPSIA information can be obtained at www.ICGtesting.com
Printed in the USA
BVOW051231160312

285364BV00003B/42/A